Baseball Defensive Drills

by Rod Delmonico, M.Ed.

Head Baseball Coach, University of Tennessee

MASTERS PRESS

Library of Congress Cataloging-in-Publication Data

Delmonico, Rod, 1958–
    Baseball defensive drills / by Rod Delmonico.
       p.   cm.
    ISBN 1-57028-110-6
    1. Baseball—Training.   2. Baseball—Defense.   I. Title.
  GV875.6.D445   1997
  796.3357'24—dc21   96-52747
                                          CIP

Cover design by Kelli Ternet
Cover photographs © Nick Myers
Interior photographs by Sarah Huff and Nick Myers

Published by Masters Press
A division of NTC/Contemporary Publishing Group, Inc.
4255 West Touhy Avenue, Lincolnwood (Chicago), Illinois 60712-1975 U.S.A.
Copyright © 1997 by Rod Delmonico
Printed in the United States of America
International Standard Book Number: 1-57028-110-6

00 01 02 03 04 05 VL 20 19 18 17 16 15 14 13 12 11 10 9 8 7 6 5 4 3

Foreword

In baseball, scoring runs is important. But as important as it is for a team to score runs, its ability to prevent the other team from scoring is just as significant.

Good defense doesn't just happen. A strong pitching staff helps, but even a future Cy Young Award winner can't stop the other team from hitting the ball, and the actions that take place after the ball is hit can mean the difference between an out or a run, or a win or a loss.

Rod Delmonico has built the University of Tennessee baseball program into a national power, and he has done it with both offense and defense. In this book that coaches at all levels can use, he outlines a regimen of drills that touch on all aspects of defensive play. He leaves no stone unturned in preparing every player at every position to play defense, from the basic fundamentals of blocking a ball in the dirt to double relays and cutoffs from the outfield to preparing the entire infield to get the lead runner at third after a bunt.

There is no doubt that hitting and offense are important segments of baseball, but a team that is physically and mentally prepared to execute defensively will win more games than it loses.

Skip Bertman, head coach, Louisiana State University
1991, 1993 and 1996 national champion

Acknowledgments

I feel indebted to several individuals who have made this book possible. I would like to thank Masters Press, especially Tom Bast, Holly Kondras and Kim Heusel, for their support during all phases of this project and making it a success. I would also like to thank the many players who posed for the photos that made this book possible. I am also very grateful for Janie Cormack who typed the manuscript, and finally, I would like to thank my family, my wife, Barb, and my sons, Tony, Joey and Nicky, for their support in all phases of my life.

Credits

Cover Photos © Nick Myers
Inside Photos by Sarah Huff and Nick Myers
Cover Design by Kelli Ternet
Edited by Kim Heusel
Inside graphic reproduction by Suzanne Lincoln
Text Layout by Kim Heusel

Introduction

In this wonderful world of video tapes and high-tech gadgetry, baseball coaches can count themselves blessed. The marketplace is loaded with all kinds of superlative wares with which to teach hitting, pitching, baserunning, fielding and just about everything else.

At Tennessee we have no compunction about using anything that works. We make use of many gadgets in helping our hitters get the most out of their quickness, strength and natural aptitudes. We have also found defensively that by using the padded baseball gloves for different drills we have seen a drastic improvement in our infielders as well. It is important, we believe, to spend countless hours out on the field working different stations to help hold our defensive skills over a period of time.

In this day and age of coaching crazes, coaches are looking for incredible drills to enhance their team's performance. We have evolved from the '50s and '60s when very few clinics, coaching tapes, books and videos were available, to a new world of full high-tech coaching. Coaches are looking for an edge to teach fundamentals and techniques to produce another Mike Piazza or the next state championship.

There is no doubt that having a few clear-cut drills to go along with your system of teaching will enable you to get the most out of your players. Today we have all kinds of aides to help a coach teach hitting, pitching, fielding, bunting, outfield play and baserunning. Some will work both indoors and outside to enhance practice.

The book is broken into five main chapters: pitching, infield, outfield, catching and team drills. As you will see in each chapter, the drills help break down each particular position to enable the player to get a well-rounded development of skills. When you get to team drills, you will notice that it is a rapid-fire simulation of repetition of the same drill over and over for a short period of time. It is much more important to work on a specific drill 10 to 20 minutes several times over the course of a week versus the old fashioned idea of working on it for an hour and a half until you get it right. This way the player does it continuously and, as we all know, repetition is the mother of skill.

Each drill in the book is designed to work on every aspect of the defensive game. In the last chapter, we put it all together so that as you look at the big picture, we develop a team made up of several positions that are fundamentally sound. I believe that a team that is fundamentally sound will have the opportunity to win every day and build on the basic fundamentals that will enhance the ability to win a national or state championship or even that Little League championship in the community.

"This is an oustanding book for coaches and players. It is great for every level of baseball."

Jim Morris, Head coach, University of Miami (Fla.)
1994 Baseball America Coach of the Year

Table of Contents

1 — Pitching 1

  Inside Pick Drill 2
  P-F-P Drill 4
  Pitcher's Rotation Drill 6
  Left-Handed Pitcher's Pick Drill 8
  1-6-3 Drill 10
  Pitcher's Reverse Pick Drill 12
  Pitcher's Bunt Defense Drill 14
  Tri-Pick Station 16
  Tennis Can Drill 18
  Double Plays 3-6-1 20
  Balance Position Leg Swing 22
  Right-Hander's Pick Play First Base 24

2 — Infield 27

  Slow Roller 28
  Double Play Drill 30
  Quick Tag Drill 32
  First Base Dirt Ball Drill 34
  Short-Hops Drill 36
  Quick Hands Drill 38
  Play-at-the-Plate Drill 40
  Backhand Drill 42
  First Base Picks 44
  First Baseman Double Plays 46

First Baseman Pickoff Drill 48
Padded Glove Double Play Drill 50
Padded Glove Drill 52
Triangle Double Play Feed Drill 54
Infielders' Dive Drill 56
Ball Overhead Sprint Drill 58

3 — Outfield 61

Line Drive Gap Drill 62
Back or In Drill 64
Rolling Catch Drill 66
Play-in-the-Sun Drill 68
Lost Ball Drill 70
Drop Step and Go Drill 72
Reverse Pivot Drill 74
Dive Drill 76
Wall Drill 78
Do-or-Die Drill 80
Outfield Communication 82
Rapid-Fire Communication Drill 84

4 — Catching 87

Quick Feet, Quick Hands Drill 88
Rapid Pop-Up Drill 90
Throwing To Second Drill 92
Catcher's Bunted Ball Drill 94
Dry Block Drill 96
Blocking Dirt Balls Drill 98
Quick Release Drill 100
Framing Drill 102
Catcher's Bent-Leg Slide Drill 104
Third Strike Ball in the Dirt 106
Catcher's Picks to First 108
Catcher's Picks to Third (with a runner on third) 110

5 — Team Drills 113

Push Drag Drill 114
Bunt Defense Drill 116
Plays at the Plate Drill 118
First and Third Defensive Drill 120
Pop Fly Communication Drill 122
Team Drills I 124
Team Drills II 126

Rundowns (Rapid-Fire) Drill 128
Double Cutoffs and Relays Drill 130
Volunteer Relay 132
Bunt Defense Runner on First 134
Bunt Defense with Runners on First and Second 136
Bunt Defense Pick at Second 138
Crash Bunt Defense 140
Horizontal Toss and Catch Drill 142
Call and Catch Drill 144
The "Z" Ball Drill 146
Catcher's Play at the Plate 148

Key to Diagrams Found in This Book

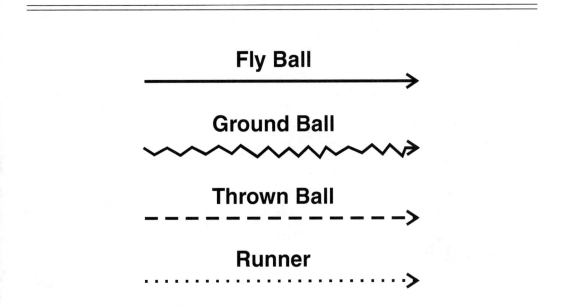

Fly Ball

Ground Ball

Thrown Ball

Runner

1
Pitching

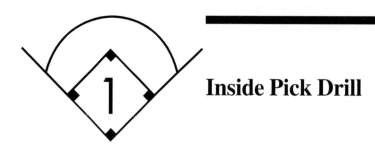

Inside Pick Drill

◆ Purpose of Drill

This drill is used to give the pitcher adequate practice in executing the inside pick drill.

◆ Equipment

Infield area, baseballs, batting helmets

◆ Implementation

1) Have the middle infielders take their position with a pitcher on the mound.

2) Position a runner at second base.

3) The pitcher will come set, kick using the inside move and throw to either the second baseman or shortstop covering which has been predetermined.

4) The infielders will rotate back and forth one at a time with the second baseman and then the shortstop covering to allow the drill to run smoothly.

◆ Key Coaching Points

1) It is important that the pitcher look as natural as possible as he kicks and pivots inside and throws to second base.

2) The kick needs to be a slow kick, deliberate with one motion toward second base.

3) This is a timing play that needs to be repeated many times to allow the infielders and pitchers to be in rhythm.

Inside Pick Drill

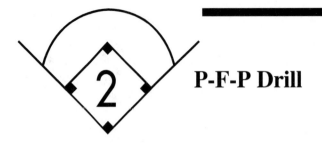

P-F-P Drill

◆ Purpose of Drill

This drill is used to teach the pitcher how to receive a ball after he has thrown to the plate using correct mechanics.

◆ Equipment

Grassy area, infielder area, pitchers mound, baseballs, fungo.

◆ Implementation

1) Have a coach position himself 60 feet away with a fungo baseball and shagger.

2) The pitcher will go through his windup simulating a thrown ball, getting into proper fielding position to receive a batted ball hit by the coach.

3) He will then field the ball and throw to a first baseman covering first base.

4) Have the coach hit line drives, one hoppers and ground balls, to simulate different types of batted balls back at the pitcher.

◆ Key Coaching Points

1) For safety purposes, I suggest younger players use the incrediball by Easton when hitting line drives back at the pitcher for safety purposes.

2) The incrediball by Easton is also a ball you can use to hit a hard line drive back at the pitcher which would avoid injury if he failed to catch the ball.

3) It is important that the coach use a first baseman with this drill so that the pitcher gets practice not only catching the ball, but also throwing to first base which completes the play.

4) Again, the incrediball will allow the coach to hit a hard line drive back at the pitcher so that he works on adapting to a hard line drive or ground ball.

P-F-P Drill

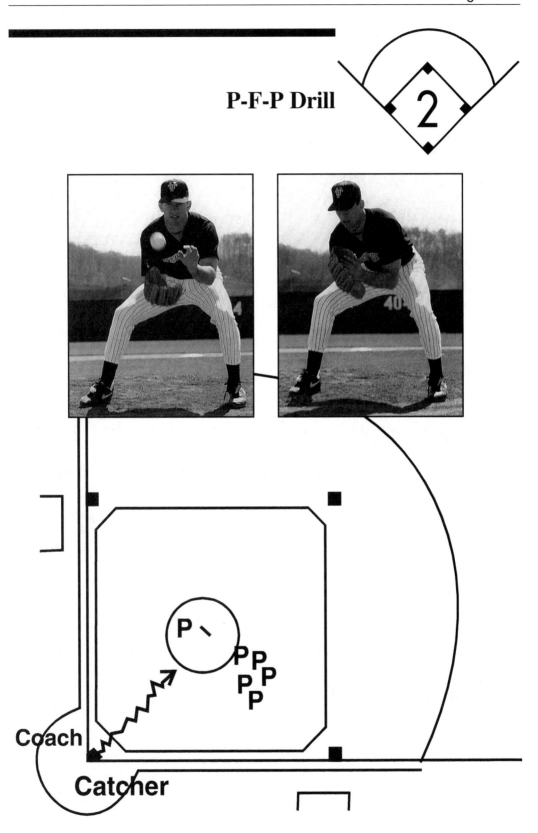

Pitcher's Rotation Drill

◆ Purpose of Drill

To teach and practice the proper rotation needed to execute a curveball or slider.

◆ Equipment

Baseball bullpen area.

◆ Implementation

1) Have the pitcher get on the mound in the bullpen or baseball field.

2) The catcher needs to take his position in front of home plate making the distance between them about 40 feet.

3) The pitcher gets to his stride position from the stretch. He wants to spread out more than shoulder width apart.

4) He will then rotate his weight back to his back foot and proceed to throw the breaking ball to his catcher, without taking a step forward.

◆ Key Coaching Points

1) Make sure that he gets his elbow above his shoulder.

2) He wants to follow through and finish with his arm beside his lead leg.

3) The pitcher needs to have proper rotation and good arm speed to produce an adequate breaking ball.

Pitcher's Rotation Drill

Left-Handed Pitcher's Pick Drill

♦ Purpose of Drill

This drill is designed to teach the left-handed pitcher how to execute properly the pickoff move.

♦ Equipment

Baseballs, infield area (first base side), pitcher's mound.

♦ Implementation

1) Position a left-handed pitcher on the pitcher's mound with a baseball.

2) Position a player at the 45-degree angle between home and first base.

3) Have a player take his position at first base.

4) The pitcher will kick and then step at the 45-degree angle and throw the ball at the player positioned between first and home.

5) Next have the pitcher kick and step at the 45-degree angle but throw to the first baseman.

♦ Key Coaching Points

1) When the pitcher is on the mound have him look at first base then kick at a 45-degree angle, step toward the 45-degree angle and then throw to first base.

2) The pitcher must drive his lead shoulder (right) toward the 45-degree angle or player positioned between home and first.

3) Make sure the pitcher has a slow leg kick and is under control as he attempts the pickoff.

Left-Handed Pitcher's Pick Drill

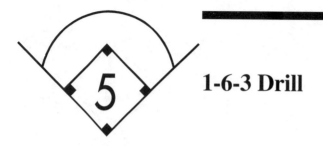

1-6-3 Drill

◆ Purpose of Drill

To allow the pitchers and infielders to work on turning the double play on a ball hit back to the mound.

◆ Equipment

Infield area, baseballs, fungos

◆ Implementation

1) The coach will position himself at home plate with a fungo and baseballs and a shagger.

2) The pitcher will position himself on the mound ready to throw the ball to the catcher.

3) The shortstop will take his normal position at double play depth ready to receive a throw from the pitcher.

4) The coach will hit a ground ball back to the pitcher after he has thrown the ball to the catcher allowing the drill to simulate game conditions.

5) After the pitcher has fielded the ball he will use the proper technique in adjusting his feet, throwing to second and starting a double play.

6) Next, the shortstop will receive the throw and throw to the first baseman covering first to complete the double play.

◆ Key Coaching Points

1) Remember it is important for the coach to have a ball in his hand and toss it up and hit it back to the pitcher when the thrown ball from the pitcher hits the catcher's mitt.

2) The coach should hit some balls softly so that the pitcher must leave the mound to field and determine whether or not he has a play at second or if he must go to first just to get an out.

3) The coach also needs to mix in a few balls right or left, one-hoppers and hard ground balls to give the pitcher practice fielding different types of batted balls.

1-6-3 Drill

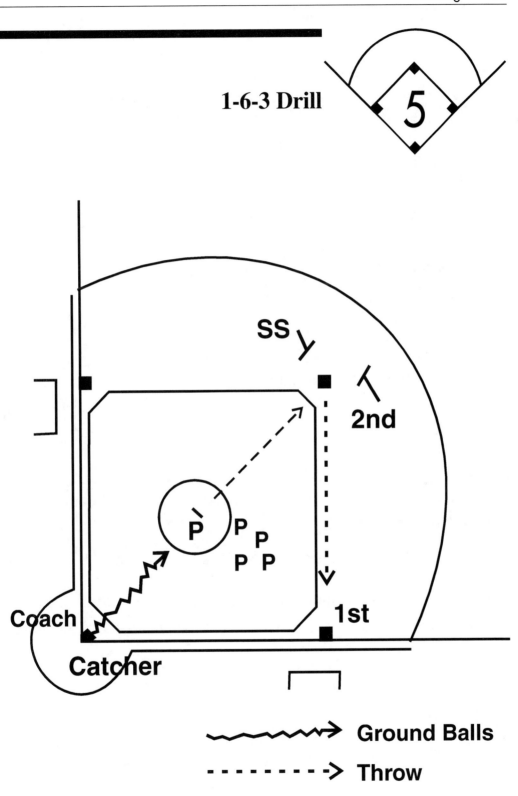

Ground Balls

Throw

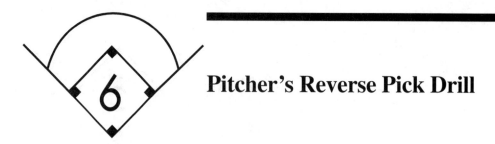

Pitcher's Reverse Pick Drill

♦ Purpose of Drill

To teach the pitcher how to execute a reverse pivot at second base.

♦ Equipment

Infield area, baseball, base

♦ Implementation

1) Have the pitcher take his position on the mound in the set position.

2) Position a base runner at second base with the middle infielders at their respective positions.

3) The pitcher will reverse pivot and throw to the second baseman covering second.

♦ Key Coaching Points

1) This is a timing play that needs to be practiced so that the players become familiar with each other.

2) If the runner is back in time, the pitcher doesn't have to throw the ball.

3) The middle infielder must break first, then the pitcher will throw to second.

Pitcher's Reverse Pick Drill

Pitcher's Bunt Defense Drill

◆ Purpose of Drill

To teach the pitchers the proper technique in executing the bunted ball in front of the mound.

◆ Equipment

Infield area, baseballs

◆ Implementation

1) Have two pitchers take their position on the mound, one to the right of the mound and one to the left.

2) The pitchers will kick, go through their windup and simulate throwing a ball to the plate.

3) A coach positioned at home plate will toss a ball down the third-base line and first-base line for each pitcher to field and set his feet ready to throw to first base and third base.

4) Position a player at third and first so that the pitchers can work on fielding a ball and throwing to first and third base.

◆ Key Coaching Points

1) You can also involve your catchers in this play and allow them to pounce on the ball, working on fielding a ball down the third-base line or first-base line that is not bunted far enough out in front of the plate.

2) Also, have two coaches or managers at home plate, one to toss a ball up the third-base line and another to toss a ball up the first-base line in order to get accuracy on both throws.

3) It is important for the coach to roll balls down the lines to simulate all types of bunted balls in a bunting situation. This is a much more difficult play for the pitcher to make.

Pitcher's Bunt Defense Drill

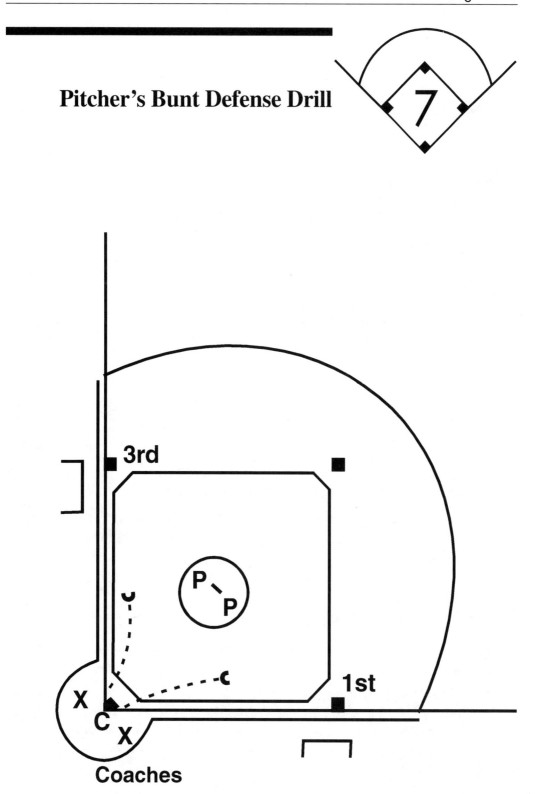

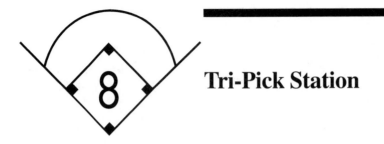

Tri-Pick Station

♦ Purpose of Drill

To have the pitchers get the proper repetition of pickoffs to first, second and third using the correct technique.

♦ Equipment

Pitching mound, infield area, baseballs

♦ Implementation

1) Have three pitchers take positions on the mound, one in the center, one on the right and one on the left of the mound, respectively.

2) The pitcher in the center will do a reverse pivot and pick at second base.

3) The pitcher on the left side of the mound will kick from the set position and pick at third base with a third baseman covering.

4) The pitcher on the right side will kick and pick at first base, regardless of whether he is a right- or left-handed pitcher, to a first baseman covering.

5) Each pitcher will make one throw and then rotate to the next line or station.

♦ Key Coaching Points

1) This allows your pitchers to work on picking to the three bases in a short period of time.

2) For safety purposes, have the pitcher take a ball to the mound as opposed to the third baseman or shortstop or catcher throwing back to the mound which could cause someone to over throw and hit someone else.

Tri-Pick Station

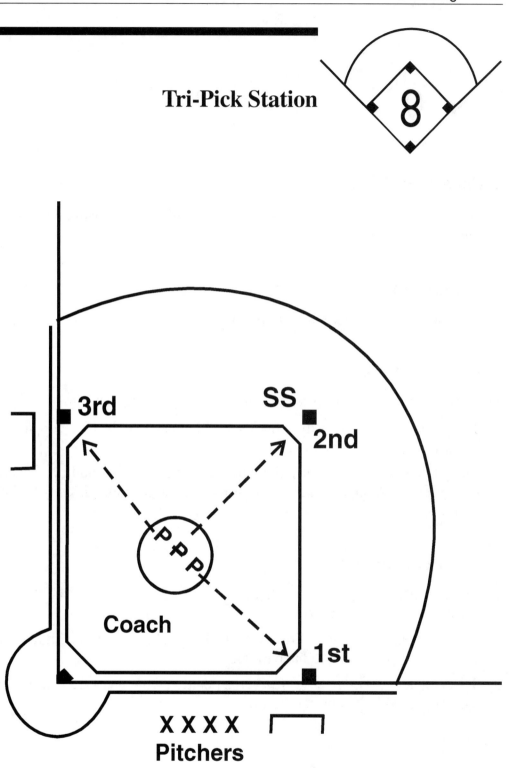

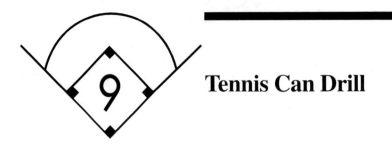

Tennis Can Drill

◆ Purpose of Drill

To teach the pitcher how to throw a curveball properly using the correct rotation and technique.

◆ Equipment

Tennis ball can, grassy area in the outfield

◆ Implementation

1) Have the pitchers pair up with each group having a tennis can.

2) The pitchers need to position themselves approximately 15 feet apart directly across from each other.

3) The pitchers will simply grip the tennis can at the bottom and flip it using the correct rotation to make the tennis can go end over end directly to their partners.

◆ Key Coaching Points

1) Make sure that the pitcher gets his elbow above his shoulder as he flips the tennis can end over end to his partner.

2) Have the group back up a little so that each pitcher can step with his lead foot as he flips the can to his partner.

3) This will help develop the correct wrist position which will aid in throwing a curveball with the correct rotation.

Tennis Can Drill

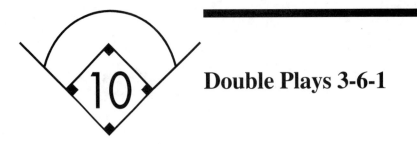

Double Plays 3-6-1

♦ Purpose of Drill

To teach the pitcher how to get over and cover first base to complete the 3-6-1 double play.

♦ Equipment

Infield area, fungos, bat

♦ Implementation

1) Have the first baseman and shortstop assume their positions, ready to receive a ground ball and throw.

2) Position the pitchers between home and first about 15 feet off the line in foul territory.

3) Have one pitcher assume his position on the mound and go through his windup and throw a baseball to the catcher shagging for the fungo hitter.

4) Position a coach at home plate who will then hit a fungo to a first baseman either to the left or right so that the first baseman must travel several feet away from the base.

5) He will then catch the ground ball and throw to the shortstop and then the shortstop will throw to the pitcher covering first base to complete the 3-6-1 double play.

♦ Key Coaching Points

1) Make sure that you hit ground balls in game-like conditions, left or right so that the first baseman must move laterally.

2) It is important that the pitcher go through his windup, throwing a pitch to a catcher shagging so that it is a game-like drill.

3) He must then break in a straight line from the mound to first base and getting in position to cover first base.

4) If you have more than one first baseman or shortstop have them rotate turning at their position.

Double Plays 3-6-1

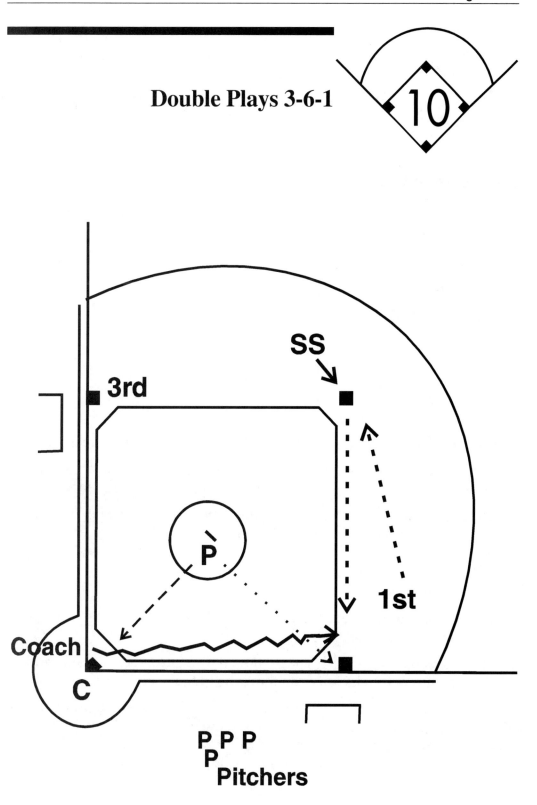

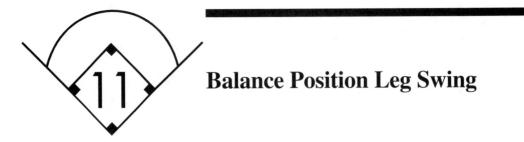

Balance Position Leg Swing

◆ Purpose of Drill

To teach the pitcher how to have the proper balance while throwing to the plate and using his legs effectively.

◆ Equipment

Baseballs, bull pen area

◆ Implementation

1) Have the pitcher assume the balanced position, ready to throw to the plate with the ball in his hand.

2) Have a catcher assume his position ready to receive a throw from the pitcher.

3) Have the coach standing right beside the pitcher with his hand holding his knee aiding him in being able to hold his position for three seconds.

4) The player will then ride his legs to the plate using the proper mechanics and arm swing while throwing a fastball to a catcher.

◆ Key Coaching Points

1) This is a drill used to teach the pitcher the importance of a balanced position and riding his legs to the plate.

2) To make sure the pitcher is able to hold the balanced position for three to four seconds before kicking and throwing to the plate.

3) After he has done this several times, let him go through his full windup, then stop at the balanced position for three seconds with the coach there to help aid and then break his hands, and throw to the plate.

Balance Position Leg Swing

Right-Hander's Pick Play First Base

♦ Purpose of Drill

This drill is designed to teach the right-handed pitcher how to execute the proper pickoff move to first base.

♦ Equipment

Baseballs, infield area, first-base side, pitchers mound

♦ Implementation

1) Position a right-handed pitcher on the pitcher's mound with a baseball.

2) Position a player at first base ready to receive a throw. Have players take their position at first base.

3) The pitcher will kick and throw and then step toward first base using the proper footwork and throwing to the first baseman.

4) Place the extra pitchers right behind the pitcher's mound where they can be ready to rotate in to work on throwing to the first baseman and the player diving back into the base.

♦ Key Coaching Points

1) It is important that the pitcher steps toward first base as he positions his feet in order to throw to the base.

2) The arm swing should be a short arm swing where the pitcher takes the ball directly out of his glove and goes up and over ready to throw with a short, quick snapping motion.

3) It is important that the pitcher be accurate, quick and not try to overthrow here. A short, quick snapping throw is the key.

Right-Hander's Pick Play First Base

2
Infield

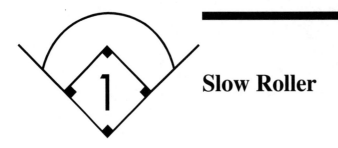

Slow Roller

♦ Purpose of Drill

To teach the infielders the proper technique in fielding the slow roller.

♦ Equipment

Infield area, fungo baseballs

♦ Implementation

1) Have the infielders take their positions.

2) Position a coach at home plate with a shagger.

3) The coach will start with the third baseman, hitting a slow roller and then watching to see if he fields it correctly and then throws to first.

4) He will then hit to the next third baseman or move to the shortstop if there is only one third baseman.

5) The coach should try to hit and coach at the same time to not slow down the drill.

♦ Key Coaching Points

1) The coach needs to explain the technique of fielding and throwing before doing this drill.

2) Have the coach hit both high-bouncers and balls that hug the ground.

3) It is important that the coach hit slow rollers a little left and right to teach the infielder to react to different types of slow rollers.

Slow Roller

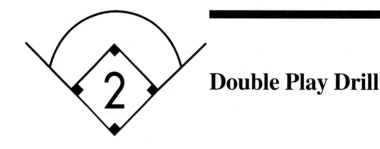

Double Play Drill

♦ Purpose of Drill

To teach the infielder the correct way to turn the double play using the proper footwork.

♦ Equipment

Infield area, ATEC flip machine, baseballs

♦ Implementation

1) Position the ATEC flip machine just in front of second base so that it flips a ball to the second baseman receiving a throw at second base.

2) Line up the second basemen at second base ready to start the drill.

3) Position the first baseman at first base or you can put a sock net halfway between first and second for the second baseman to throw into.

4) The coach will turn on the machine and the second basemen will go one at a time using the correct footwork while catching the ball then throwing to the first baseman or sock net.

5) After the second baseman has thrown to first base, the coach will then rotate the machine on to the second base side of second base lining it up for a flip to the shortstop that will receive the ball and throw to first base.

♦ Key Coaching Points

1) Make sure that the infielders get to the base under control ready to receive a flip.

2) For the drill to work smoothly, it is important to have two to three middle infielders doing the drill.

3) By using a sock net, this drill can also be used without any first baseman allowing the middle infielders to get a great workout on turning the double play without having to have a coach hit fungos or a first baseman to receive throws.

Double Play Drill

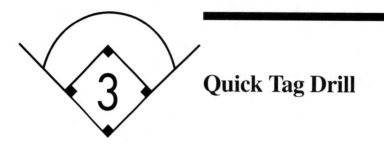

Quick Tag Drill

◆ Purpose of Drill

To work on the proper footwork and mechanics for making a tag play at second base.

◆ Equipment

Rookie pitching machine, baseballs and infield area

◆ Implementation

1) Set up a pitching machine in front of the pitcher's mound.

2) Have your middle infielders get about six feet away from the base ready to break for the base to receive a throw.

3) On command, the coach will direct the players to break toward second and then he will feed a ball in the machine.

4) The middle infielder will get in position, catch the ball and make the proper tag.

◆ Key Coaching Points

1) The player needs to get away from the base and then break toward the base and set up. This makes the drill game-like.

2) After he catches the ball, the middle infielder should take the glove straight to the first base side of the base for the quick tag.

3) The coach needs to mix in some bad throws such as one-hoppers, balls thrown low and high so the infielder can react appropriately.

4) As the infielder receives the throw he should take the glove directly to the base ready to tag the runner out.

Quick Tag Drill

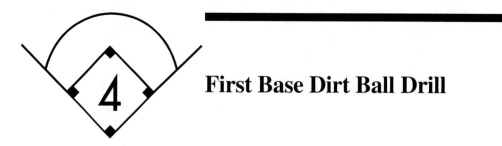

First Base Dirt Ball Drill

◆ Purpose of Drill

To teach the first baseman how to use the correct mechanics when catching a ball that is thrown in the dirt.

◆ Equipment

First base area, base, baseballs

◆ Implementation

1) Position a first baseman in front of the bag ready to receive a throw.

2) Position a coach behind the pitcher's mound with several baseballs.

3) The coach will throw balls in the dirt with the first baseman using the proper technique in receiving the throws from the coach.

◆ Key Coaching Points

1) It is important to mix in different types of hops: short hops, long hops, in-between hops. This allows the first baseman to get several different types of throws.

2) The coach also needs to work the fielder's forehand and backhand to allow each player to work on both his strengths and weaknesses.

3) A variation of the drill would be for the coach to use a pitching machine, positioning it in the shortstop area so that the first baseman receives a throw that is more game-like.

First Base Dirt Ball Drill

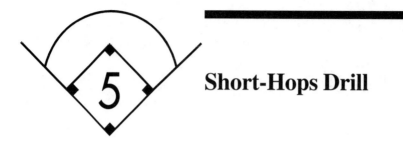

Short-Hops Drill

♦ Purpose of Drill

To teach infielders the proper mechanics in catching the long and short hops.

♦ Equipment

Infield area, baseballs

♦ Implementation

1) Have the players pair off about 8-10 feet apart.

2) While one player is preparing to throw a short hop the other is in proper fielding position.

3) When the partner catches the ball he simply throws a short hop back to the other fielder.

♦ Key Coaching Points

1) Make sure that the fielders bend their knees and reach out with both hands to receive the ball.

2) It is important that the fielders mix in different types of hops — some short, some longer.

3) Try to throw the ball so that the infielder doesn't have to move left or right.

Short-Hops Drill

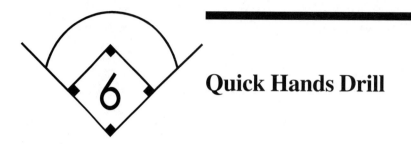

Quick Hands Drill

◆ Purpose of Drill

To teach infielders to catch and throw the ball quickly.

◆ Equipment

Baseball, glove, grassy area

◆ Implementation

1) Have the players pair up.

2) The players should stand across from each other about 20-25 feet apart.

3) The players will throw to each other, trying to get the ball out of their gloves and throw back to their partners as quickly as possible.

◆ Key Coaching Points

1) Make sure the players have a firm grip on the baseball before they throw it.

2) The players need to shuffle their feet in order to line up their lead shoulder in the direction they are throwing the ball.

3) The players should try to throw the ball chest high.

Quick Hands Drill

Play-at-the-Plate Drill

♦ Purpose of Drill

To teach the infielders the correct technique in receiving a ground ball and throwing to the plate in an infield in position.

♦ Equipment

Infield area, baseballs, fungo

♦ Implementation

1) Position the infielders in an "in" position ready to receive a ground ball.

2) Position a coach at home plate with a fungo and several baseballs.

3) The catcher needs to be at home plate ready to receive a throw from the infielder after he catches the ball.

4) The coach will hit a ground ball starting with the third baseman; the third baseman will receive the ball and throw to the catcher. At that time, the coach will hit a ground ball to the next available infielder.

♦ Key Coaching Points

1) A variation of the drill is for the catcher to make a simulated tag on a catcher coming in on a non-forced play.

2) The catcher can then receive the ball in a force situation, adjusting his feet and then throwing to first base to complete the double play.

3) This drill works not only the infielders but also your catchers on making plays at the plate.

Play-at-the-Plate Drill

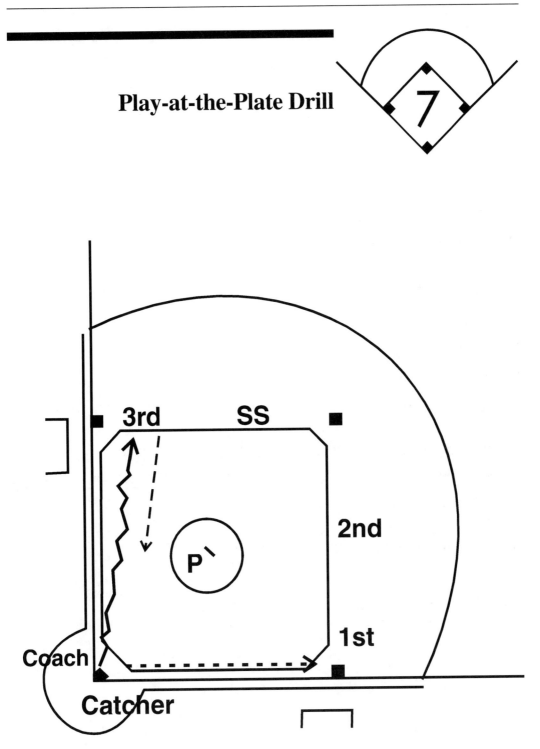

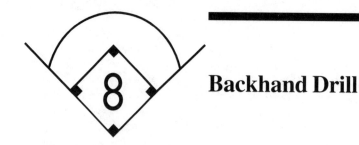

Backhand Drill

♦ Purpose of Drill

To allow the player to develop the proper technique in catching a ball using the backhand method.

♦ Equipment

Baseballs, infield area

♦ Implementation

1) Have the players pair up into groups approximately 10 feet apart in the infield area.

2) Each player will roll a ball to his partner's backhand side.

3) The player will catch the ball and then roll a ball to his partner's backhand side.

♦ Key Coaching Points

1) This drill should go for approximately 3-5 minutes.

2) Make sure that the players use proper fielding techniques especially toward the end of the drill when they get tired.

Backhand Drill

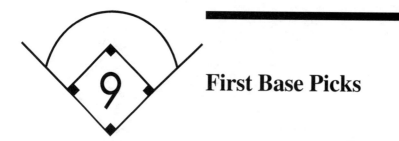

First Base Picks

♦ Purpose of Drill

To work on executing the quick tag at first base on a throw from the pitcher.

♦ Equipment

Infield area, baseballs and helmets

♦ Implementation

1) Have the pitcher and first baseman take their positions with the pitcher ready to attempt a pickoff at first.
2) The runner will get his lead with the rest of the runners in foul territory.
3) The pitcher will throw to first base trying to pick off the runner.
4) The first baseman will catch the ball and execute the correct tag.

♦ Key Coaching Points

1) After catching the ball, the first baseman should go directly to the infield side of the base to make a tag.
2) Instead of using a pitcher the coach can stand on the mound or make throws for the first baseman to catch and make a tag.
3) The coach should mix in some short hops and throws off line so the first baseman can work on different types of throws.

First Base Picks

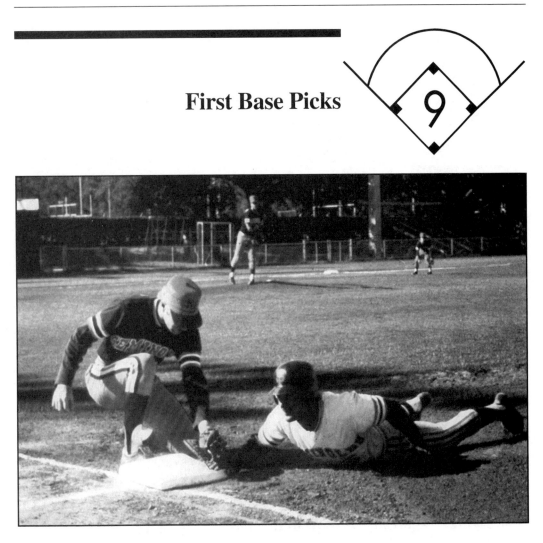

First Baseman Double Plays

◆ Purpose of Drill

This drill is designed to give the first baseman repetition in fielding ground balls and throwing to second base and then recovering and receiving a throw at first base to complete the double play.

◆ Equipment

Fungo, baseballs, infield area

◆ Implementation

1) Have the first baseman start in his normal position back behind first base ready to receive a ground ball.

2) Position a coach at home plate with baseballs and a shagger.

3) Position a shortstop at second base ready to receive a throw.

4) The coach will hit a fungo, the first baseman will field it and throw it to the shortstop. As the shortstop catches the ball, he will execute the proper footwork to get ready to throw to first base.

5) As the first baseman recovers, he will receive the throw from the shortstop.

6) Now have the first baseman get on the base as if he was holding a runner as a coach throws the ball in the air. He will break off the base into his normal fielding position even with the bag, ready to receive a ground ball.

7) After fielding the ball, he will throw the ball to the shortstop and get back to first base ready to receive a throw if at all possible.

◆ Key Coaching Points

1) Move the first baseman left to right. Try to hit him choppers so that he gets all types of ground balls during this drill.

2) The first baseman will receive some balls left to right which will prohibit him from getting back to the base. This is where the pitcher would break and cover first base.

First Baseman Double Plays

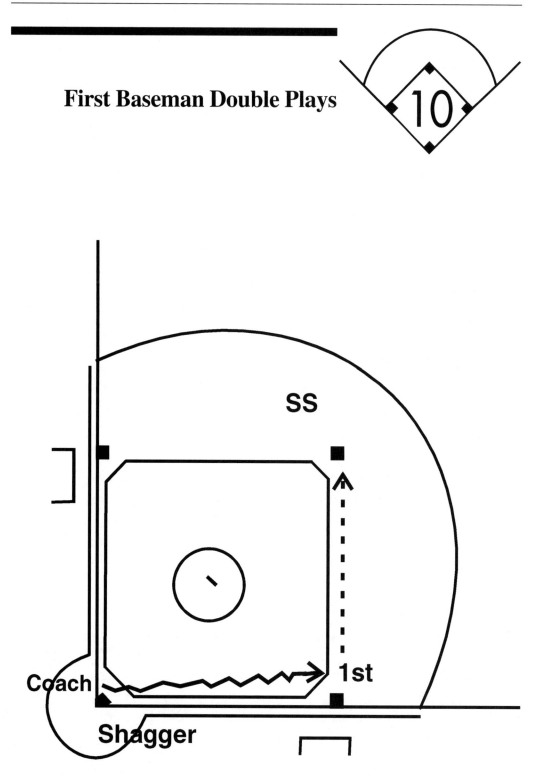

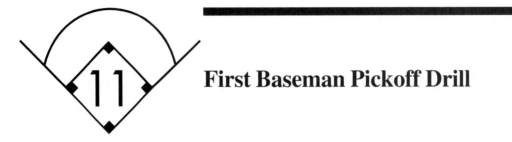

First Baseman Pickoff Drill

◆ Purpose of Drill

To allow the first baseman to practice receiving a throw from a left-handed pitcher and then throwing to second base to get the runner which left first base on the first movement from the left-handed pitcher.

◆ Equipment

Infield area, baseballs, bases

◆ Implementation

1) Have the left-handed pitchers line up behind the mound with one pitcher assuming the set position with a baseball ready to throw to first base.

2) Have the first baseman take his position at first base ready to receive a throw.

3) Position a shortstop at second base ready to receive the throw from the first baseman after he catches the ball.

4) The pitcher will kick and throw to the first baseman with the first baseman catching the ball and then throwing it to the shortstop on the infield side of second base.

◆ Key Coaching Points

1) Make sure that the first baseman, after seeing the direction of the throw, cuts the distance between him and the pitcher's mound. In other words, go get the baseball.

2) It is important for the first baseman to shuffle his feet and point his shoulder in the direction of second base as he completes his throw.

3) The first baseman should try to throw the ball on the infield side of second base.

4) To simulate game situations, make sure the shortstop makes a phantom tag at second.

First Baseman Pickoff Drill

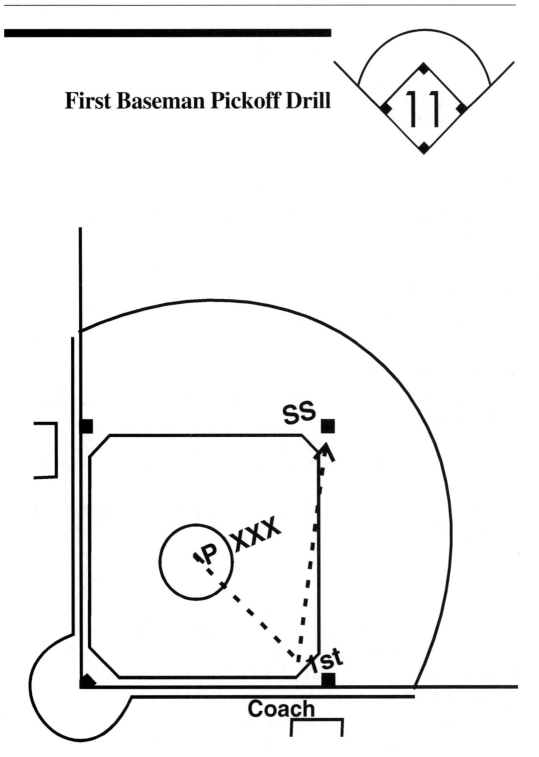

Padded Glove Double Play Drill

♦ Purpose of Drill

To teach the infielder how to catch the ball with two hands when turning a double play.

♦ Equipment

Padded glove, baseballs, second base area

♦ Implementation

1) Have a coach roll ground balls from around the pitcher's mound area to infielders as they work on double play balls.

2) The coach can also back up to home plate using a fungo, hitting to the shortstop while the second baseman uses the padded glove to turn double plays.

3) After the second baseman has turned double plays using the padded glove, the coach will now flip-flop and have the shortstop use the padded glove as he hits fungos to the second baseman.

♦ Key Coaching Points

1) Make sure the infielder using the padded glove gets to the bag under control with both hands up.

2) As he reaches he must catch the ball with two hands, making sure to get the lead out and completing the double play.

3) The coach can add a first baseman to the drill so that the infielder must catch the ball and move his feet and throw to first base.

Padded Glove Double Play Drill

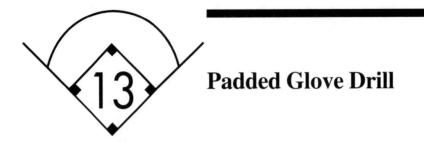

Padded Glove Drill

♦ Purpose of Drill

To teach the infielder how to field the ground ball with soft hands using a padded glove.

♦ Equipment

Padded glove, baseballs, fungo

♦ Implementation

1) Have the infielders take their positions wearing the padded glove.

2) The coach will hit a fungo, the infielder must field the ball using the padded glove and throw to first base.

3) The coach will hit balls left to right which force the infielder to move his feet, get in front of, reach out to receive the ball, give with it, cradle it in and throw to first base.

♦ Key Coaching Points

1) Make sure the infielder reaches out, gives with it, catches the ball with two hands, with the throwing hand on top.

2) The coach needs to hit not only ground balls, but one-hoppers and also balls left and right to allow the infielder to work on different chances that he might have.

Padded Glove Drill

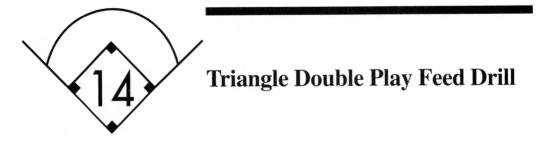

Triangle Double Play Feed Drill

♦ Purpose of Drill

To work on getting the ball out of the glove and making the proper feed to the shortstop or second baseman. This drill will allow the infielders to work on different feeds in a short period of time.

♦ Equipment

Baseballs, grassy area or infield area

♦ Implementation

1) The coach will divide the infielders into groups of three.

2) Each group will make a triangle approximately six to eight feet apart.

3) The infielders will now work on giving forehand or backhand flips to their partner going either to the right or left.

♦ Key Coaching Points

1) Make sure that the infielder, as he flips the ball, gets his glove out of the way so that his partner can see the baseball coming.

2) Make sure that the infielder doesn't try to be too quick and that he catches and gets the ball out of his glove making an accurate throw to the partner.

Triangle Double Play Feed Drill

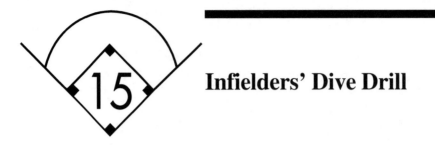

Infielders' Dive Drill

◆ Purpose of Drill

To teach the infielders how to dive either to the forehand or backhand to catch a baseball.

◆ Equipment

Baseball, grassy area

◆ Implementation

1) Have the infielders go one at a time with a coach approximately 30 feet away ready to throw a baseball.

2) The coach will first start throwing toward the infielders' forehand sides and then work them to their backhands.

3) The coach will throw a ball where the infielder must leave his feet and dive for the ball.

4) After the infielders have worked on catching the ball to their forehand, the coach will then work them on their backhand.

◆ Key Coaching Points

1) Make sure that you throw the ball so the infielder must leave his feet and reach out and make the catch and then slide with both arms extended on the ground.

2) It is important that you throw balls that the infielder must reach for and sometimes not be able to catch. This allows the infielder to build up his distance laterally.

Infielders' Dive Drill

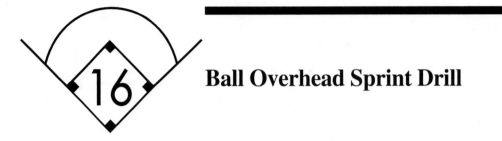

Ball Overhead Sprint Drill

♦ Purpose of Drill

To teach the infielder how to go back on a fly ball and make the catch either forehand or backhand.

♦ Equipment

Baseballs, grassy area

♦ Implementation

1) Line up the infielders in a line beside a coach; every infielder has a ball.

2) The infielders will start sprinting straight back looking over their right shoulders; the coach will throw a ball and the infielders will run and make the catch.

3) After the infielders have caught the ball over their right shoulders the coach will throw it over the left shoulders for them to make the catch.

4) The next part to the drill is to have the infielder run looking over his right shoulder; the coach will throw it over the opposite shoulder.

5) The infielder will now look over his left shoulder and the coach will throw it over his right shoulder. He must rotate, sprint and catch the baseball.

♦ Key Coaching Points

1) This will allow the infielder to learn to catch the ball over either shoulder sprinting back into the outfield.

2) It is important that when the coach throws the ball over the opposite shoulder that the infielder pick up the ball as quickly as possible.

3) When rotating and going to get a baseball, after the infielder has rotated to the opposite shoulder he must go directly to the ball.

Ball Overhead Sprint Drill

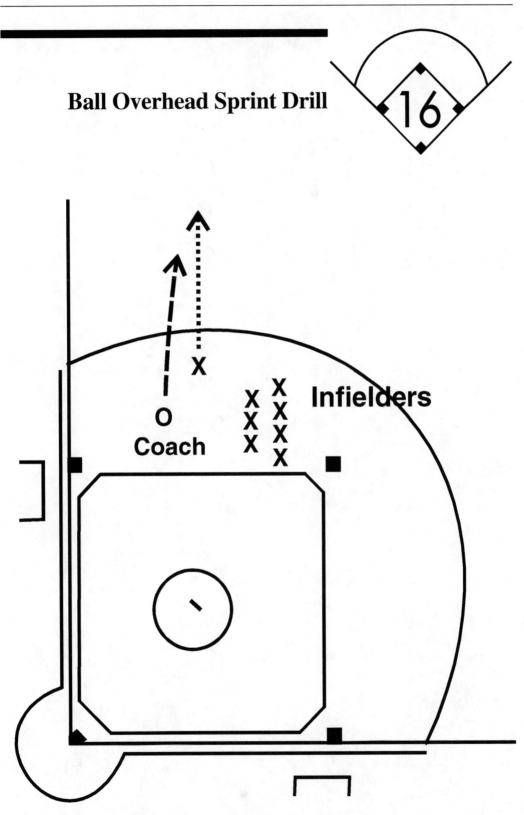

3
Outfield

Line Drive Gap Drill

◆ Purpose of Drill

To teach the outfielder the proper technique in running and catching a line drive either to his forehand or backhand while on the run.

◆ Equipment

ATEC rookie pitching machine, baseballs, outfield area

◆ Implementation

1) Have the outfielders line up going one at a time approximately 60 yards away from a coach stationed on the right-field line.

2) The coach will set up a rookie pitching machine that will throw line drives either left or right of the outfielder.

3) On the coach's command the outfielder will start sprinting to his forehand while the coach leads him with a line drive in order for him to make the catch by reaching out and snagging the line drive.

4) All the outfielders will go in one direction whether it is forehand or backhand, then the coach will set the line drive so they will now sprint back across the outfield working on either their forehand or backhand.

5) After the player has caught the ball he must come to a stop, set his feet and throw back into a cutoff man or a shagger who is standing beside the coach.

◆ Key Coaching Points

1) Make sure that the coach allows the outfielder to run several steps before he has to make a catch, which simulates game conditions.

2) It is also important that the outfielder be put in a position to make a difficult catch where it is a do-or-die situation — either he catches it or he doesn't. The more difficult the catch the more game-like the drill becomes.

3) Another version of the drill is for the coach to throw the ball instead of using the machine. Remember that the distance must be shortened to about 30 yards between the coach and outfielder.

Line Drive Gap Drill

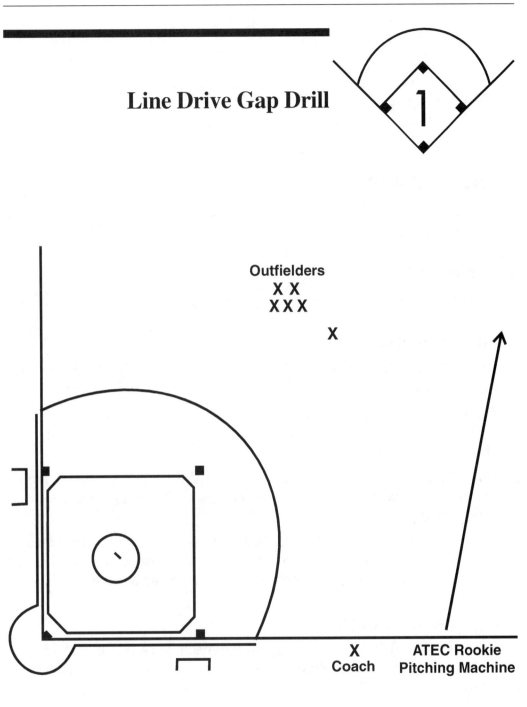

Outfielders
X X
X X X

X

X
Coach

ATEC Rookie
Pitching Machine

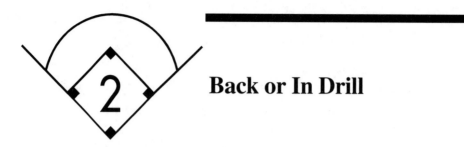

Back or In Drill

◆ Purpose of Drill

To teach the outfielder to come in on a line drive or drop step and go back on a line drive.

◆ Equipment

ATEC rookie pitching machine, baseballs, grassy area

◆ Implementation

1) Have the outfielders position themselves approximately 60 to 70 yards away from a coach that is stationed on the right- or left-field line.

2) The coach will set the machine for a line drive in front of the outfielder forcing him to sprint in and catch the ball that is hit directly at him or charge it and catch it on the run.

3) Have the players go one at a time and after making the catch, gather themselves and throw the ball into the cutoff man or the shagger who is shagging for the coach.

4) After the players have worked on the line drive ball that they must charge in on and make the catch, the coach can work on line drives hit directly over the head that they must sprint back on and make a catch.

◆ Key Coaching Points

1) It is important that the coach position the machine so that it will throw a line drive a little left or right of the outfielder as he comes in or goes back on the ball to make a catch.

2) The coach can also get a little closer and throw the ball as opposed to using a machine or fungo.

3) If the coach throws the ball, have the players start running in before the coach throws the ball either right or left. Also, he must shorten the distance between him and the player which would also aid in accuracy and repetition.

Back or In Drill

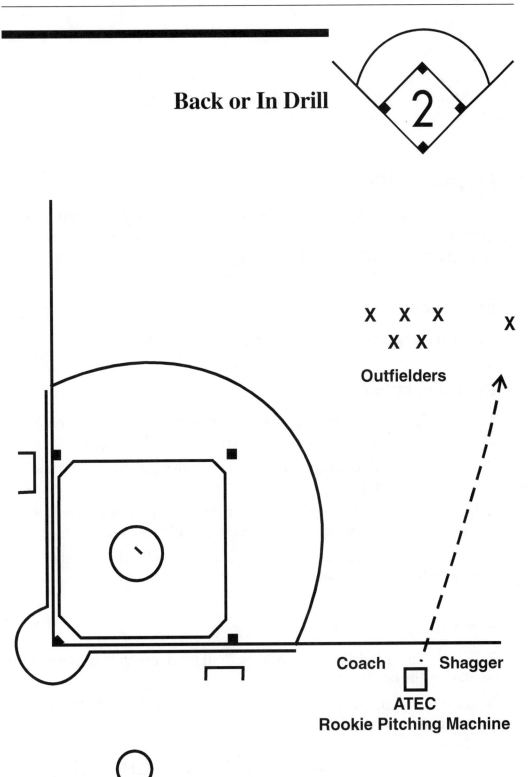

Outfielders

Coach   **Shagger**

ATEC
Rookie Pitching Machine

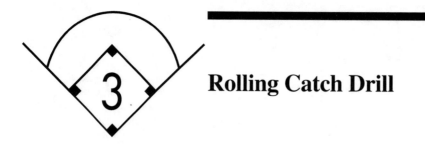

Rolling Catch Drill

♦ Purpose of Drill

This is a fun drill to teach the technique of rolling on the ground, getting up, picking up the baseball and making a catch. It is a drill which will work on advancing a player's athletic ability and agility.

♦ Equipment

Outfield area, baseballs, fungo, or pitching machine

♦ Implementation

1) Have the outfielders get approximately 100 feet away from the coach that is positioned on the right-field line with a fungo and shagger.

2) The outfielders will go one at a time as the coach tosses the ball up and hits it to the outfielders.

3) When the coach makes contact, the outfielder must do a forward roll on the ground, pop to his feet, find the baseball and make the catch.

4) The outfielder needs to react to whatever type of ball is hit, whether it is a ground ball, line drive, semi-line drive, or pop-up.

♦ Key Coaching Points

1) This is a drill designed for fun, but also will teach the athlete some agility in playing the outfield.

2) Make sure you hit the pop-up high enough to give the outfielder enough time to make a forward roll, pop to his feet, find the baseball and make the catch.

3) For accuracy purposes, it might be better to use a machine where you can set the height of the ball and make sure you give the outfielder enough time to complete the drill.

Rolling Catch Drill

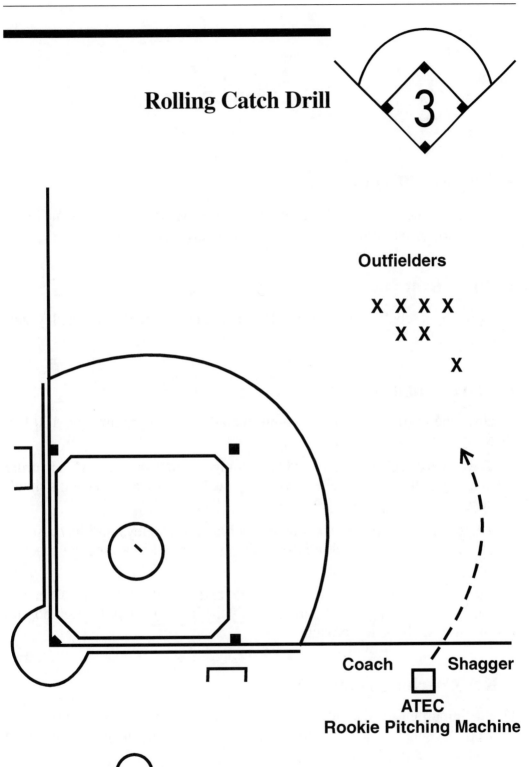

Outfielders

X X X X
X X
X

Coach   Shagger

ATEC
Rookie Pitching Machine

Play-in-the-Sun Drill

♦ Purpose of Drill

To teach the outfielder the proper technique in using sunglasses and glove to assist him in catching a fly ball on a sunny day.

♦ Equipment

Fungo, baseballs, or ATEC pitching machine, outfield area, Oakley sunglasses

♦ Implementation

1) Have the outfielders line up going one at a time approximately 100 feet away from a coach.

2) The coach can either use an ATEC pitching machine or a fungo bat in order to hit fly balls to an outfielder with the sun directly over the coach's shoulder.

3) The outfielder will use sunglasses such as the Oakleys and his baseball glove to aid him in blocking the sun's rays so that he can see the baseball and make the catch.

4) The coach needs to hit balls left or right and over the outfielder's head so that he gets practice in catching not only the line drive but the high pop-up and also the balls left or right.

♦ Key Coaching Points

1) It is important for the outfielder not only to use sunglasses but also to get work in using his baseball glove to help shield the sun in order to make the catch.

2) It is important that the coach not only hit line drives but balls overhead or ground balls to simulate game conditions.

Play-in-the-Sun Drill

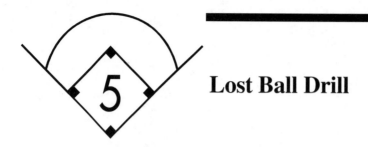

Lost Ball Drill

♦ Purpose of Drill

To teach the outfielder to find the ball after he has lost it because of the sun or other reasons.

♦ Equipment

Fungo, Incredible balls (by Easton), grassy or outfield area

♦ Implementation

1) Have the players line up about 100 feet away with their backs to the coach.

2) The coach will line up with a fungo, incredible balls and a shagger.

3) The coach will toss the ball up and hit a high pop-up close to the outfielder.

4) After he hits the ball he will yell "Ball!" and the outfielder must find it.

♦ Key Coaching Points

1) Make sure you use incredible balls by Easton in case you hit a line drive directly at the fielder.

2) You can also use this drill on a sunny day and have the outfielders use sunglasses.

3) The coach can also hit semi-line drives for quicker reactions.

Lost Ball Drill

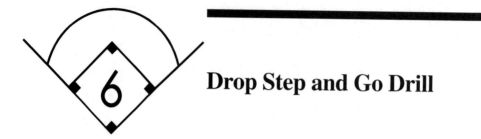

Drop Step and Go Drill

♦ Purpose of Drill

To teach the player how to drop step and go back and catch a ball hit behind him.

♦ Equipment

Grassy area, outfield, fungo and balls

♦ Implementation

1) Have the players line up with one player beside the group lined up.

2) Position a coach about 180 feet away with a fungo, balls and shagger.

3) The coach will throw the ball up and hit the ball behind the fielder's head.

4) The player will drop step and go back to catch the ball hit over his head.

♦ Key Coaching Points

1) If the coach fails to hit the ball over the player's head, have the player react to the ball.

2) It is important for the outfielder not to break until the ball is hit. This will teach him to read the ball off the bat.

Drop Step and Go Drill

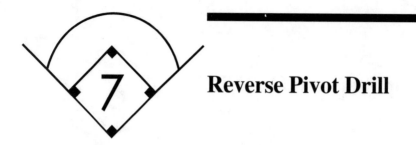

Reverse Pivot Drill

◆ Purpose to Drill

To teach the outfielder how to reverse pivot and catch the ball after he has turned the wrong way.

◆ Equipment

Fungo, balls, grassy area or outfield area

◆ Implementation

1) Line up the outfielders about 150 to 180 feet away.

2) Position a coach with a fungo, balls and shagger ready to hit fly balls over the outfielder's head.

3) When the coach tosses the ball up, have the feeder take a drop step back to his right or left side.

4) The coach will hit the ball on the opposite side of where the player opened up.

5) This will cause the player to reverse pivot, find the ball and make the catch.

◆ Key Coaching Points

1) Make sure that the coach hits the ball on the opposite side of the direction the outfielder breaks backward.

2) As the outfielder reverse pivots make sure that he finds the ball quickly and then proceeds to make the catch.

3) When the outfielder reverse pivots he will have a tendency to slow down. He must keep running at some pace until he identifies how hard the ball was hit.

Reverse Pivot Drill

Dive Drill

♦ Purpose of Drill

To teach the outfielder the proper technique in making a diving catch in the outfield.

♦ Equipment

Grassy area, baseballs

♦ Implementation

1) The outfielders will line up going one at a time with a coach kneeling approximately 20 to 30 feet away.

2) On the coach's command the outfielder will sprint in at a 45-degree angle either right or left of the coach. The coach will pitch the ball in the air approximately two to three feet off the ground and the outfielder will dive and attempt to catch the ball before it hits the ground using the proper technique.

3) It is important for the coach to have some sense of timing so that the outfielder must leave his feet to have any chance to catch the ball.

♦ Key Coaching Points

1) It is important to teach the outfielder the proper technique in catching the ball when he must leave his feet whether he does a head-first slide or a bent leg slide before attempting to do his drill.

2) The outfielder must concentrate on extending his arms straight out (both arms), and as he catches the ball, slide on top of the ground much like a head-first slide keeping his arms from rolling up underneath him.

3) For safety purposes, when teaching the bent leg slide to catch a fly ball, have the outfielders remove their cleats and slide in their sock feet until they feel comfortable with the drill to avoid injury.

Dive Drill

8

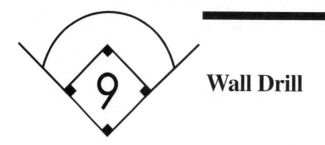

Wall Drill

♦ Purpose of Drill

To teach the outfielder how to position himself to play the ball off the wall.

♦ Equipment

Outfield area, warning track, wall or fence, baseballs

♦ Implementation

1) The coach will line up the outfielders approximately 20 to 25 yards off the fence with the coach approximately 30 yards away from the outfielders.

2) On command, the coach will throw the ball over the outfielder's head allowing the outfielder to square up and position himself to catch the ball rebounding off the wall.

3) The coach can also throw balls that will cause the outfielder to go up against the wall to catch the ball using the proper technique.

4) After the coach has worked the outfielder going over his right shoulder, he will rotate the group to the left side so that they can now work on catching the ball over their left shoulders.

♦ Key Coaching Points

1) Make sure that the outfielders use the proper technique of bracing their body with one hand as they go up against the wall to catch the ball up high on the wall.

2) Another version of the drill is to put a cutoff man into position so that when the outfielder catches the ball off the wall, he must shuffle his feet and throw to hit the cutoff man.

3) Once he hits the warning track the outfielder needs to know how many steps he has before coming in contact with the wall. Normally it is three to four strides on the average distance of a warning track. Once he hits the track he has three to four strides before he gets to the wall.

Wall Drill

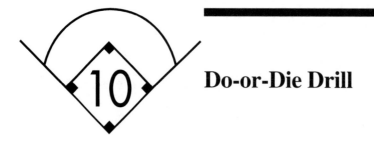

Do-or-Die Drill

♦ Purpose of Drill

To teach the outfielder the proper technique in fielding a ground ball in a do-or-die situation and throwing to the plate or another base.

♦ Equipment

Fungo, baseball field or outfield area, baseballs

♦ Implementation

1) Have the outfielders line up in center field going one at a time with a coach on the right-field line with the outfielders in center field.

2) The coach will hit a fungo to one outfielder at a time instructing him to catch the ball on the outside of the glove foot, crow hopping and then throwing to a cutoff man or a netting device that can be used as a shagger. The coach can either hit one-hoppers or mix in different types of ground balls that an outfielder may receive.

♦ Key Coaching Points

1) The coach needs to hit balls left or right of the outfielder so that he can take a quick 45-degree angle and cut off the distance between him and the ball and work on rounding the ball off and throwing to a cutoff man.

2) The coach can also put a sock net up that will allow the outfielder to throw to a specific target, one either in the air or by one-hopping it so that the outfielder can work on accuracy. The coach needs to work on giving the outfielder the opportunity to work not only on one-hoppers, but also hard-hit balls right at him so he can work on a variety of ground balls to simulate throwing situations in a game.

Do-or-Die Drill

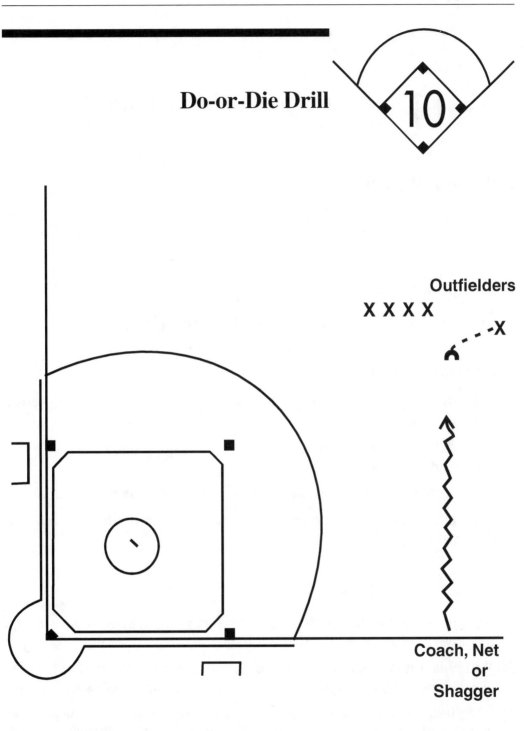

Outfielders

X X X X

- - -X

**Coach, Net
or
Shagger**

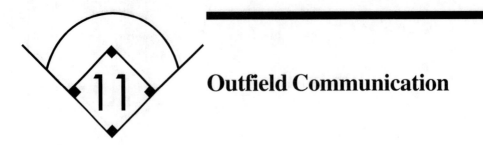

Outfield Communication

◆ Purpose of Drill

To teach the outfielders the proper communication on a pop fly in the outfield.

◆ Equipment

Outfield area, pitching machine or fungo, baseballs

◆ Implementation

1) Have the outfielders split into two groups, one in center field and the other in left-center.

2) Position a coach on the right-field foul line with a fungo or pitching machine and baseballs.

3) The coach will hit a ball between the two outfielders of each group.

4) The outfielders will use the proper communication on calling the ball and then making the catch.

◆ Key Coaching Points

1) It is important that the coach have at least six players, three in each group, to allow the players to effectively run the drill.

2) With this drill you can also hit line drives in front of the outfielders and also behind the outfielders to work on different types of balls in the gap.

3) The group in center field should always be considered the center fielder and should have priority over the catch if they call the ball first.

Outfield Communication

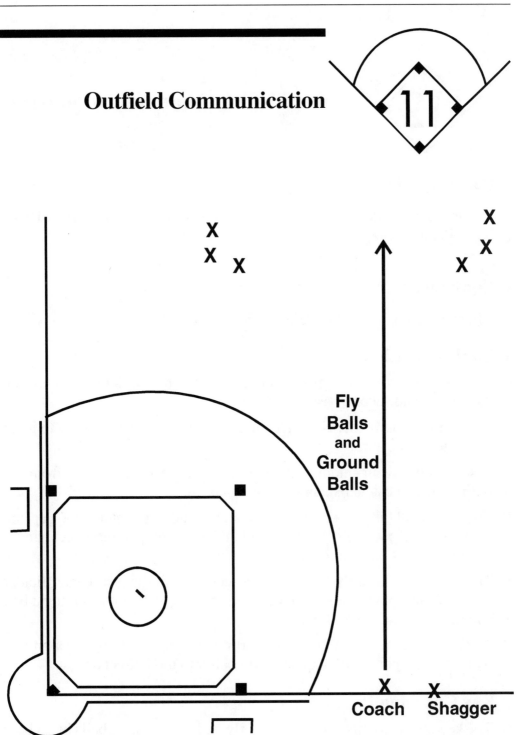

Rapid-Fire Communication Drill

◆ Purpose of Drill

To teach outfielders how to use proper angles when catching ground balls and fly balls in the gap.

◆ Equipment

Fungo, baseballs, outfield area, infield area

◆ Implementation

1) Have a coach position himself right behind the pitcher's mound between the mound and second base.

2) Position your outfielders in left, center and right with extras ready to jump in and take their turn.

3) Also, position your middle infielders ready to receive a throw from the outfield with a catcher shagging for the coach.

4) The coach will hit a ground ball between left and left-center in the gap and then outfielders will break on the ball taking the proper angle receiving it and throwing it back to the infield.

5) The coach will hit a fly ball into right-center with the next center fielder and right fielder working on the proper communication on fielding a ball and throwing back into the infield.

6) The coach will alternate back and forth and then switch hitting a ground ball into the right-center gap and a fly ball into the left-center gap.

◆ Key Coaching Points

1) The key here is to mix up the type of fly balls and ground balls hit in both gaps so that the outfielders get work on coming in on ground balls as well as going back on fly balls and ground balls to cut off the angle.

2) It is important that you have at least six outfielders so that you can get a lot of work done and keep this drill moving.

Rapid-Fire Communication Drill

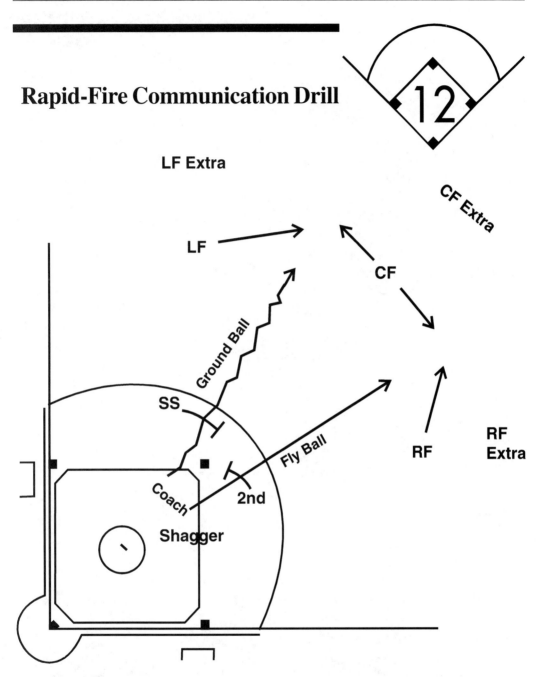

3) It would also be important to use a shortstop and second baseman who would be the cutoff man in the left-center field gap and then have another set of infielders, second and short that will field balls into the right-center gap. This will allow you to work in tandem and get more work done in a shorter period of time.

4) The coach can also use a pitching machine if he is not as accurate with a fungo to allow the drill to work more smoothly.

4
Catching

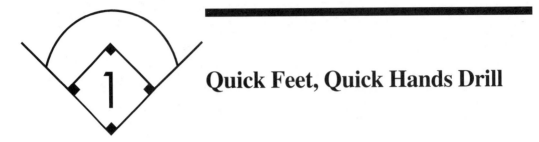

Quick Feet, Quick Hands Drill

◆ Purpose of Drill

To teach the catcher the correct footwork in receiving the ball and making the throw as quickly as possible using the proper technique.

◆ Equipment

Flip net or hanging net, grassy area, baseballs, catcher's gear

◆ Implementation

1) Have the catchers dressed in full gear, warmed up ready to play catch and throw at full capacity.

2) Have a coach position himself approximately five to six feet away right off the throwing side of the catcher at a 45-degree angle.

3) The coach will make a firm toss to the catcher, simulating a thrown ball which the catcher will receive using the proper footwork and throw into a net which is directly in front of him about six feet away.

◆ Key Coaching Points

1) It is essential that the coach toss the ball firmly in order for the catcher to receive a throw that simulates game conditions.

2) The coach also wants to work on throwing balls, inside, outside, high or low to work on all types of throws.

3) The coach wants to get as much in a straight line as possible just off the catcher's throwing side so that the catcher is receiving the flip straight on. This way, as the coach makes a firm underhand toss the catcher will receive a ball coming directly at him.

Quick Feet, Quick Hands Drill

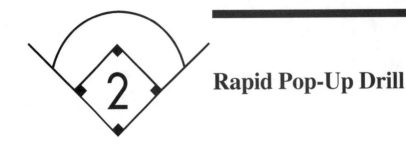

Rapid Pop-Up Drill

♦ Purpose of Drill

To teach the catcher how to catch the ball that is popped up behind the home plate area.

♦ Equipment

Baseballs, catching equipment, ATEC rookie pitching machine, home plate area

♦ Implementation

1) This drill works best if you have two to four catchers involved.

2) Squat in a catching position behind home plate.

3) The coach will set the machine so it pops up a ball behind home plate.

4) The coach will put a ball in the machine and pop a ball up to the first catcher.

5) While the ball is in the air, the coach will pop up another ball to the next catcher in a different area behind home plate.

♦ Key Coaching Points

1) Have the catchers wear their gear so they can execute under game-like conditions.

2) The ATEC rookie machine is designed so that you can simply rotate the upper part to quickly change directions of the pop-up.

3) The drill is also a great conditioner for the catchers as well.

4) You may set the machine so it will place a ball at the base of the wall. This will give the catcher practice on catching balls at the base of the wall.

5) He will then proceed to block the ball to his left and return back to his catching stance.

Rapid Pop-Up Drill

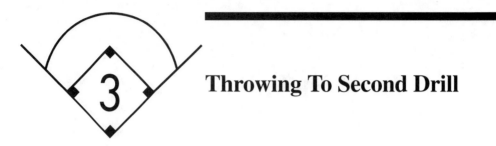

Throwing To Second Drill

◆ Purpose of Drill

To accurately teach the catcher the proper technique in throwing to second base.

◆ Equipment

Catching equipment, infield, baseballs, bases, stop watches and batting helmet

◆ Implementation

1) Have a catcher set up behind home plate in full gear.

2) Position a coach or pitcher on the mound with the ball ready to throw.

3) Position a middle infielder on second base.

4) Have the coach or pitcher throw the ball to the catcher.

5) As the catcher recovers the throw he will then throw to second.

◆ Key Coaching Points

1) Position a player in the batter's box to simulate a real game.

2) The batter should rotate from a left-handed batter to a right-handed batter.

3) The coach can use a stop watch to time the catcher's throw to second. A good time is 1.9 to 2.1 seconds for a high school or college player.

Throwing To Second Drill

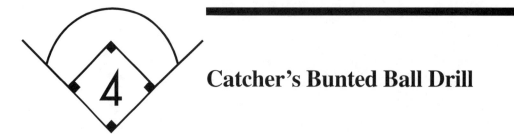

Catcher's Bunted Ball Drill

◆ Purpose of Drill

To teach the catcher how to effectively field the bunted ball or chopper hit directly in front of the plate.

◆ Equipment

Infield area, baseballs, catcher's gear

◆ Implementation

1) Have one catcher take his position behind home plate with the others lined up directly beside him in foul territory.

2) The coach will position himself directly behind the catcher. He will then toss the ball up the first- or third-base line or directly in front of the plate and the catcher will pounce on the ball, throwing it to first base.

3) The next catcher will jump in and use the proper technique in fielding a bunt and throwing to a first baseman who is covering first base.

◆ Key Coaching Points

1) This drill works better with two to three catchers going at one time. This keeps the drill moving and allows the catcher to make several throws in a short period of time working on all areas in front of the plate using the correct technique.

2) If no first baseman is available and you have three catchers, one catcher can receive throws at first base while two catchers are fielding their position, and then rotate.

3) It is extremely important that the catchers do this drill with their gear on and get used to throwing to first base with all of their gear.

Catcher's Bunted Ball Drill

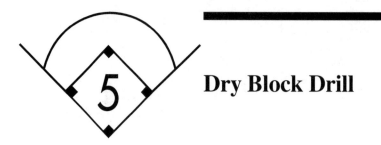

Dry Block Drill

♦ Purpose of Drill

To teach the catcher the correct technique in blocking a ball in the dirt.

♦ Equipment

Grassy area or home plate area, three baseballs, catcher's gear

♦ Implementation

1) Have the catcher assume his stance ready to block a ball in the dirt.

2) The coach will place three balls in front of the catcher approximately three feet apart.

3) The three balls will represent the ball in front of the plate as well as inside and outside of the plate.

4) On the coach's command he will point out a ball and the catcher will block that baseball using the proper technique.

5) The catcher, upon blocking the simulated ball in the dirt, will pop back up to his catching stance.

♦ Key Coaching Points

1) Make sure the catcher attacks the ball cutting the distance between him and the ball.

2) The coach can also number the balls and simply call out a number for him to block.

3) Make sure the catcher blocks with full gear on just like a game.

Dry Block Drill

Blocking Dirt Balls Drill

♦ Purpose of Drill

To teach the player the proper technique in blocking the ball in the dirt.

♦ Equipment

Grassy area or home plate area, catcher's gear, baseball or soft toss balls by Easton.

♦ Implementation

1) Set up an area either at home plate or the outfield to work on the proper technique in blocking the ball in the dirt.

2) The coach should position himself about 30 feet in front of the catcher ready to throw the ball in the dirt.

3) As the coach releases the ball the catcher will go to his knees using the proper fundamentals.

♦ Key Coaching Points

1) After the catcher has blocked the ball, have him bounce to his feet ready to throw to a base to make it game-like.

2) The catcher wants to make sure that he works on balls inside and outside as well as down the middle.

3) By using a soft ball made by Easton or tennis ball you will keep from beating up your catcher. Also, for younger players it keeps them from being afraid of the ball.

Blocking Dirt Balls Drill

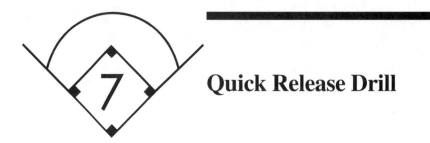

Quick Release Drill

♦ Purpose of Drill

To teach the catcher to make the quickest possible exchange from the glove to the throwing hand.

♦ Equipment

Catcher's gear, baseball, grassy area in outfield

♦ Implementation

1) Position the catchers across from each other on their right knee.

2) The catchers should be about 15 to 20 feet apart from each other.

3) The catchers will begin throwing to each other back and forth trying to get the ball out of the glove as quickly as possible.

4) The catchers want to make a quick crisp throw.

♦ Key Coaching Points

1) The catcher should rotate his shoulders so his left shoulder is pointing at his partner before he releases the ball.

2) It is important that the catcher makes the exchange of the ball from the glove to throwing hand in front of the chest area.

3) This drill will also help develop arm strength.

Quick Release Drill

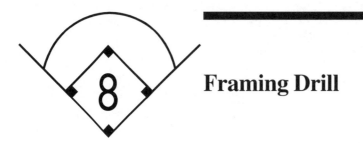

Framing Drill

♦ Purpose of Drill

To teach the catcher how to receive the ball correctly in all zones.

♦ Equipment

Grassy area or home plate area, baseballs, pitching machine

♦ Implementation

1) The catcher will take his stance behind home plate ready to receive the throw.

2) The coach will set up an ATEC rookie pitching machine about 40 feet away ready to throw to the catcher.

3) The coach will feed the machine and the catcher will receive the pitch and frame it accurately.

♦ Key Coaching Points

1) The coach needs to work on all types of pitches: inside, outside, high and low.

2) The coach needs to set up the machine so that the catcher can also work on catching balls just off the plate.

3) For older players, the coach can set the speed higher so that the catcher can work on his quickness.

Framing Drill

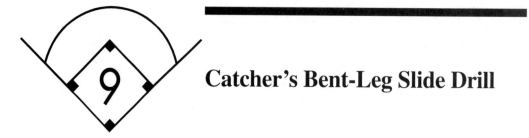

Catcher's Bent-Leg Slide Drill

♦ Purpose of Drill

To teach the catcher how to execute a catch against the fence or near the dugout area.

♦ Equipment

ATEC rookie pitching machine, baseballs, catcher's gear

♦ Implementation

1) Have the coach set the pitching machine so that the ball will come down right in front of the wall.

2) The catcher will squat down behind home-plate in his catcher's stance.

3) The coach will feed the ball into the machine and the catcher will break, find the ball and execute the bent-leg slide.

4) The coach can move the machine around so that the ball drops in front of the dugout forcing the catcher to execute the bent-leg slide in front of the dugout while avoiding running into the dugout.

♦ Key Coaching Points

1) It is better to have two to three catchers executing this drill at one time which will allow the drill to move smoothly.

2) The key point is to use a pitching machine so that you can accurately set the machine to allow the baseball to drop a foot or two in front of the wall.

Catcher's Bent-Leg Slide Drill

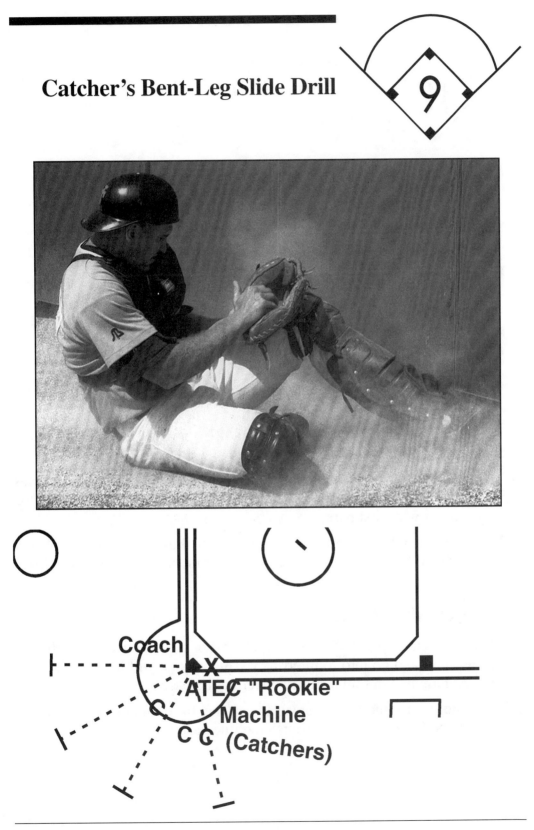

Third Strike Ball in the Dirt

◆ Purpose of Drill

To allow the catcher to work on blocking the ball in the dirt, getting to his feet and throwing the runner out at first base.

◆ Equipment

Catcher's gear, baseballs, infield area

◆ Implementation

1) The coach will be approximately 40 feet from home plate with several baseballs ready to throw to the catcher.

2) The catcher will get in his set position in full gear ready to block the ball in the dirt on a third strike pitch.

3) The coach will throw a ball in the dirt, the catcher will block it as if it was strike three and the batter had swung. He will hop to his feet, retrieve the ball and throw to first base.

4) Have the coach throws balls, left or right where the catcher must block it in foul territory, hop to his feet and throw to a first baseman covering first.

◆ Key Coaching Points

1) Make sure you throw balls off the plate left or right so that they rebound off his chest and go into foul territory. This way he will have to throw to the first baseman in foul territory covering the base.

2) It is important for the first baseman and catcher to communicate on whether they are both on the inside or outside of the base line.

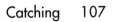

Third Strike Ball in the Dirt

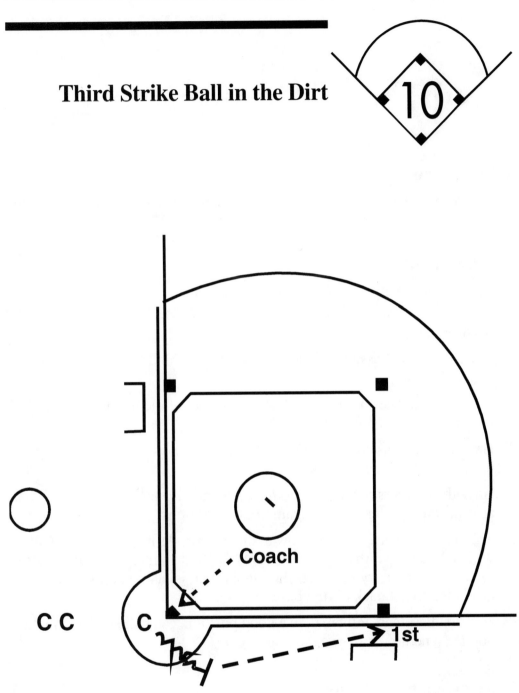

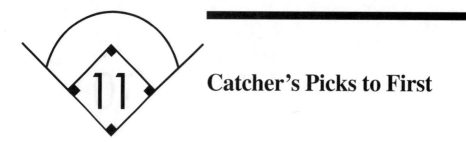

Catcher's Picks to First

◆ Purpose of Drill

To teach and to work on the correct fundamentals of picking a runner off first base.

◆ Equipment

Infield area, catching gear, baseballs

◆ Implementation

1) The catcher will assume his normal position behind home plate with full catcher's gear.

2) A coach, manager or player will stand in front of the mound with several baseballs ready to throw to the catcher.

3) Have the first baseman assume the back position as if he was playing behind a runner.

4) Have the catchers rotate, the alternate catcher will stand in the batter's box as if he was a hitter to create game-like conditions.

5) The coach or manager will throw to the catcher. As he receives the ball he will make a snap throw by adjusting his feet and pointing his lead shoulder toward first base trying to get the runner who is taking an extra lead and has failed to get back to first base.

6) The first baseman will break in a good position, catch the ball and make a pop tag, and hopefully get the runner out.

◆ Key Coaching Points

1) Have the first baseman work on holding the runner on, shuffling off and then receiving a throw and rotating to his glove side to make the pop tag on the runner as he dives back to first.

2) If the catcher possesses the arm strength, he can make a snap throw from his knees, but this must be practiced often for accuracy.

Catcher's Picks to First

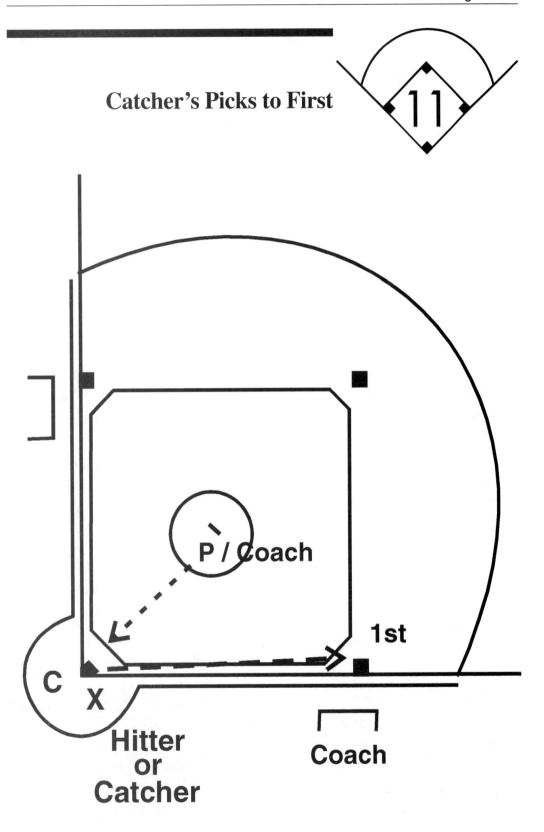

Catcher's Picks to Third (with a runner on third)

◆ Purpose of Drill

To work with your catchers on the pickoff move to third base after the catcher has received the ball.

◆ Equipment

Infield area, third base, baseballs, catcher's gear

◆ Implementation

1) Have a catcher assume his normal position in full gear behind home plate.

2) Position a coach on the pitcher's mound with several baseballs ready to throw to the catcher.

3) The third baseman will assume his normal position at third base ready to receive a throw from a catcher after he has caught the ball.

4) The coach will throw to the catcher. As the catcher receives the ball he will catch it, look at third, glance back at the pitcher as if he is going to throw back at him and then fire to the third baseman on the infield side of third base.

5) This is a timing play that needs to be worked on frequently so that the third baseman and catcher have their timing down.

◆ Key Coaching Points

1) It is important that the catcher decoy this pick by glancing at the runner and then glancing to the pitcher as if he is going to throw to the pitcher. At that time he will throw from his knees to third base on the infield side.

2) The other phase to this drill is that as the catcher receives the ball he immediately goes to the third baseman, who is covering third, on a quick snap throw to try and catch the runner breaking too far down the line.

3) Your catcher must possess adequate arm strength in order to throw from his knees on the quick snap throw after he has received the throw.

4) Have the catchers rotate being a hitter so the catcher is in a game-like situation; one catcher in the box while the other is throwing.

Catcher's Picks to Third
(with a runner on third)

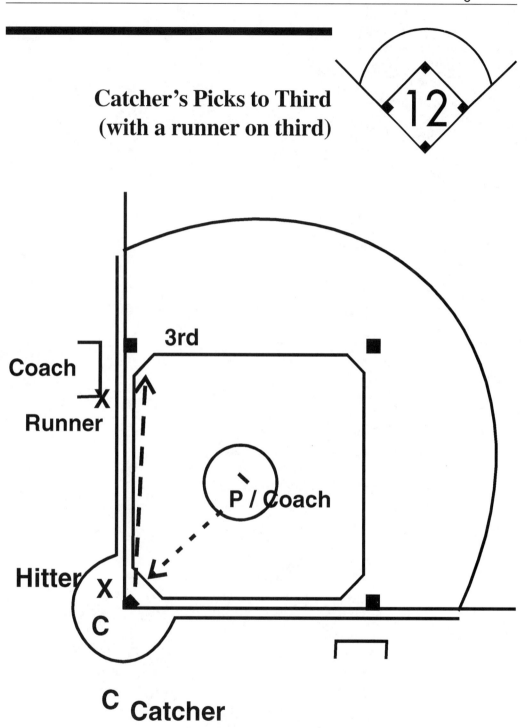

5

Team Drills

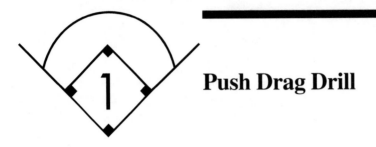

Push Drag Drill

♦ Purpose of Drill

To teach the infielders how to correctly field the bunted ball and throw to first base on the run.

♦ Equipment

Infield area, baseballs, bats, helmets

♦ Implementation

1) Have the infielders take their positions in the infield. Position a coach/pitcher or pitching machine on the mound.

2) Have the hitters go one at a time, bunting the ball either down the third-base line or pushing it toward the first-base side.

3) The infielders will field the ball using the correct technique and throw to first base hopefully in time to get the runner out.

♦ Key Coaching Points

1) It is essential that the infielders do not move until the hitters show bunt.

2) This is a great drill not only for the defense to work on fielding base-hit bunts, but it also is a great drill for the offense to work on dragging or pushing for a base hit.

3) This drill can be used indoors in a gym or in an indoor turf area when live scrimmaging is not possible. This way the players can work on base-hit bunts while the position players can work on defending the base-hit bunt.

Push Drag Drill

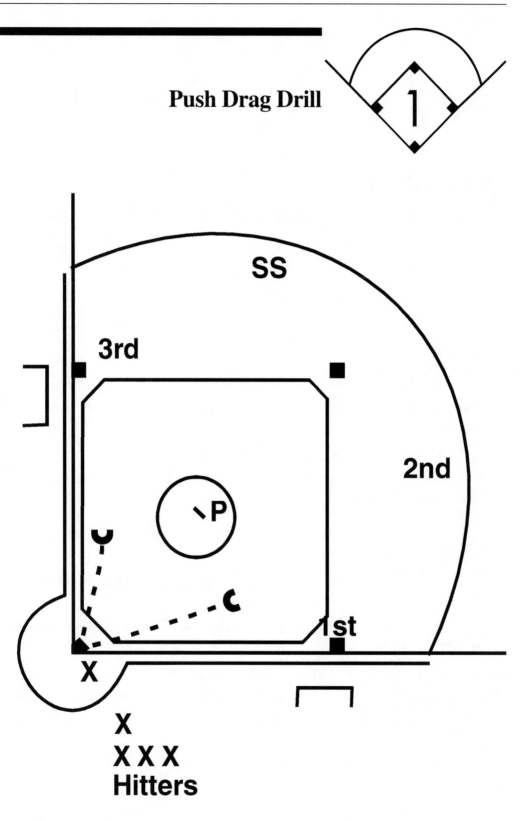

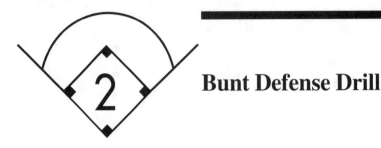

Bunt Defense Drill

◆ Purpose of Drill

To work on executing and defending the bunted ball by the offense.

◆ Equipment

Bat, balls, infield, batting helmets

◆ Implementation

1) Set up a defensive team with pitchers throwing live to bunters.

2) Start with a runner on first base and then proceed to runners at first and second.

3) Have the pitcher set and throw to the bunter.

4) The defensive squad will react to the bunted ball and throw to the appropriate base.

◆ Key Coaching Points

1) Make sure that the pitcher is ready to throw; we want the drill to be game-like.

2) You can attempt pickoff plays at first and second to keep the base runners from leaving early.

3) Challenge your defense to make sure they get an out.

4) If the offense makes a bad bunt, such as back to the pitcher, the defense should be able to get the lead runner out.

Bunt Defense Drill

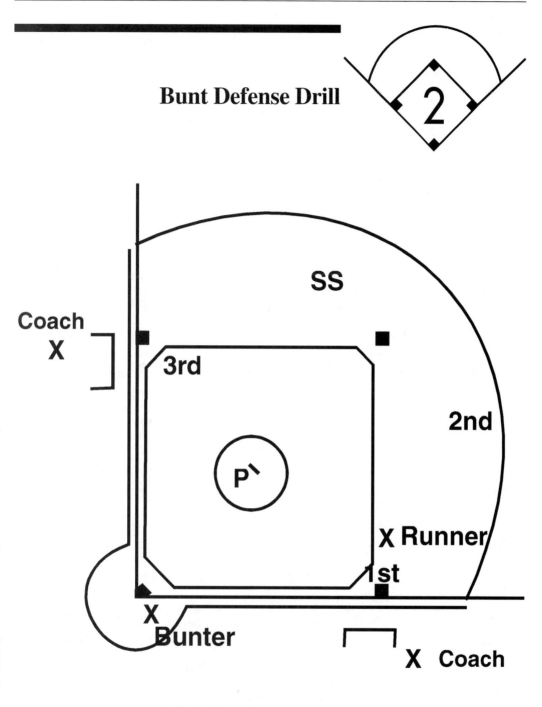

SS

Coach
X

3rd

2nd

P

X Runner

1st

X
Bunter

X Coach

XXXX Bunters

Plays at the Plate Drill

♦ Purpose of Drill

To practice throwing to the plate or third-base line.

♦ Equipment

Fungo, balls, baseball field and batting helmet

♦ Implementation

1) Put a line up on the field in all nine defensive positions.

2) Have the extra players and pitchers line up at home plate in foul territory.

3) Position a coach in front of home plate with a fungo and baseball.

4) Position a runner on second base with a normal lead.

5) When the coach hits the ball to the outfielders have the runners take off.

6) The outfielders will throw to home plate through the cutoff area.

♦ Key Coaching Points

1) You can use the following verbal communication to communicate to the cutoff man. If the catcher says nothing let it go.

2) If he says "cut" — cut the ball and hold it. He can also say "cut 4," "cut 3," "cut 2," or "cut 1," and the cutoff man will throw to the base called.

3) If he yells "relay," cut the ball and throw home.

4) Make sure that the cutoff man is in a straight line between home and the outfield.

5) It is the catcher's responsibility to get the cutoff man in a straight line. He can simply yell "left one, right two" for example.

6) Make sure that the runners don't take off too soon or it will not be game-like.

Plays at the Plate Drill

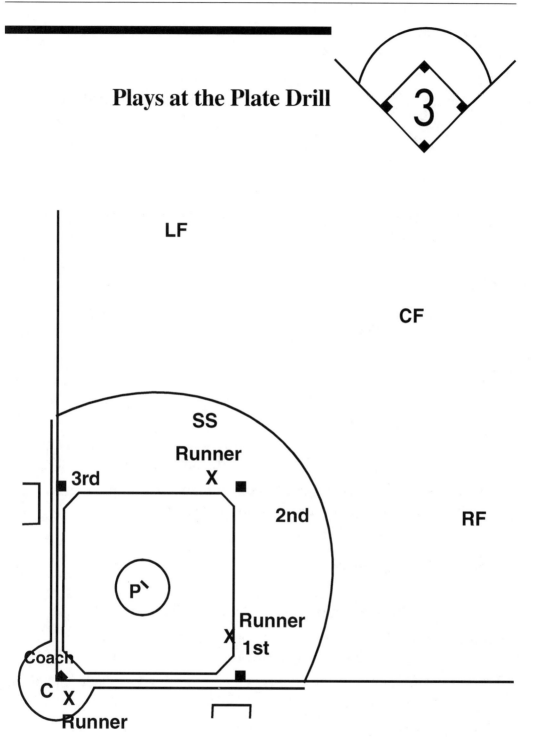

First and Third Defensive Drill

♦ Purpose of Drill

To teach the infielders to execute the proper technique in defending the first and third offensive situations.

♦ Equipment

Baseballs, infield area

♦ Implementation

1) The infielders need to take their positions with runners occupying first and third base, respectively.

2) The pitcher will start the drill by throwing from the stretch to the plate with the runners executing a predetermined offensive situation.

3) The defense will react to the offensive situation using the correct technique in defending against the offensive maneuver.

♦ Key Coaching Points

1) It is important that you put the defense in every possible offensive situation to allow them to get practice in defending the play.

2) It is important that the coach isolate one or two situations per session and work on defending that play before moving on to another situation.

3) This is a defense that needs to be executed often to allow the infielders the repetition needed to correctly defend the play.

4) To help make the drill run smoothly, the coach should have several runners lined up ready to go at first and third base.

First and Third Defensive Drill

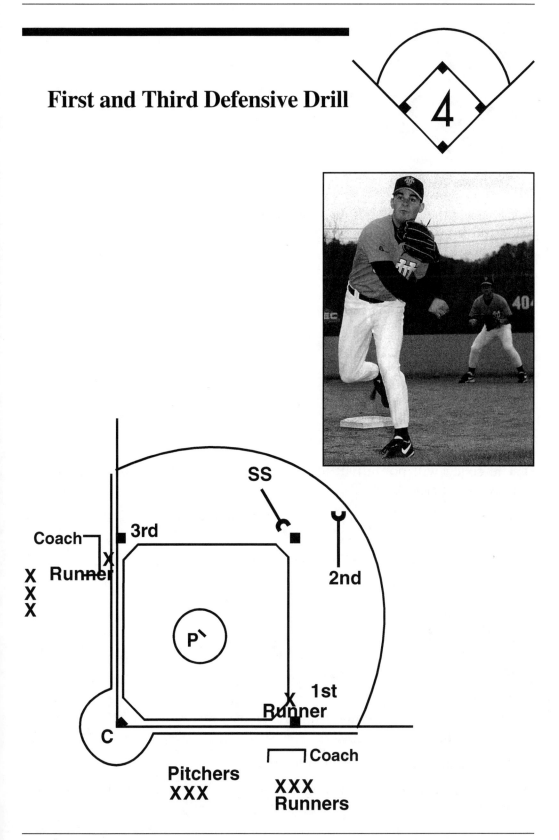

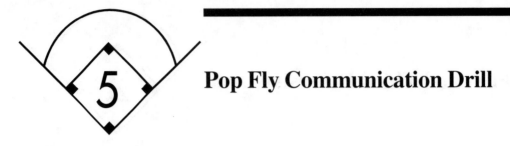

Pop Fly Communication Drill

♦ Purpose of Drill

To teach the concept of communication between infielders and outfielders during a pop-up.

♦ Equipment

Fungos, ATEC rookie machine, baseballs, baseball field

♦ Implementation

1) Position a starting lineup on the field consisting of both infielders and outfielders.

2) Have the coach set up the ATEC rookie pitching machine at home plate using real baseballs or dimple balls by ATEC.

3) The coach will pop a ball up on the right side of the diamond for the players to reach.

4) While the first ball is still in the air he can rotate the machine and pop up a ball on the left side of the diamond.

5) The next ball can be in the middle of the field for the players to call for and then catch.

♦ Key Coaching Points

1) Make sure that the fielders do not call for the ball too soon. Wait until it reaches to the top of its height.

2) The players should yell three times "I've got it", if they have enough time. This avoids players saying it simultaneously resulting in neither one hearing the other.

3) This is a great drill to execute on a windy day.

4) The coach can also use a fungo if he doesn't have access to a pitching machine.

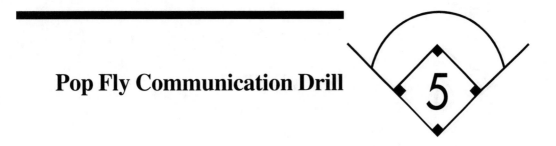

Pop Fly Communication Drill

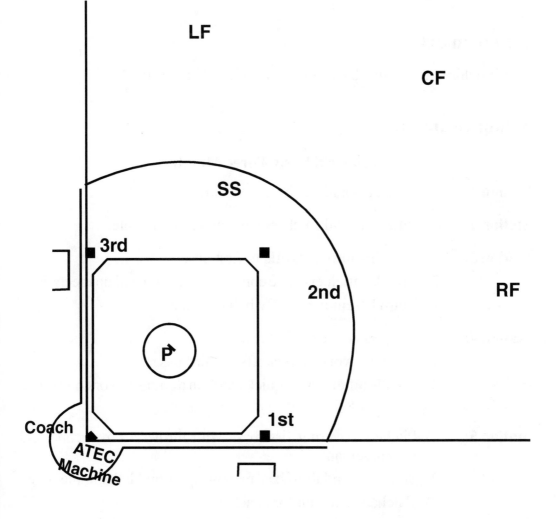

Team Drills I

◆ Purpose of Drill

To give the defensive squad repetition on the fundamentals that will be repeated over the course of a season.

◆ Equipment

Infield/outfield area, baseballs, fungos, catcher's gear

◆ Implementation

(Each Drill Lasts Three Minutes)

Station 1: 1) Infielders and catchers have slow rollers.

Station 2: 1) Infielders and catchers have plays at the plate.

Station 3: 1) Catchers have pickoffs to first base.
2) Middle infielders have communication on ball up the middle.
3) Third basemen have fly ball over the head.

Station 4: 1) Pitchers covering first base.
2) Catchers work on pickoffs to third base.
3) Middle infielders do quick hands in a circle or work on double play feeds.

Station 5: 1) Pitchers covering first base with throws from second and first baseman.
2) Shortstop and third basemen have ground balls in the hole.
3) Catchers catch up for coaches.

Station 6: 1) Pitchers, first basemen and middle infielders have 3-6-1 play.
2) Catchers and third basemen have pop-up communication.

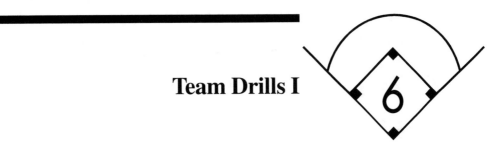

Team Drills I

Station 7:   1) Pitchers, middle infielders and first basemen have come-back-ers (1-6-3 and 1-4-3).

2) Catchers and third basemen continue communication.

Station 8:   1) Pitchers have no-step throw to first base.

2) Middle infielders have forehand and backhand.

3) Third basemen have forehand and backhand.

Station 9:   1) Pitchers, infielders and catchers have bunts with runners on first and second base.

Station 10:   1) Pitchers and middle infielders have pickoffs at second.

2) Third basemen work on short hops by throwing about 50 feet away from the bag.

3) First basemen work on short hops by throwing about 50 feet away from the bag.

4) Catchers are framing pitches.

Station 11:   1) Pitchers have pickoffs to first base.

2) Catchers are blocking balls.

3) Infielders have tag plays or pop-ups.

Station 12:   1) Infielders and outfielders have communication.

Total Time: 36 minutes

♦ Key Coaching Points

1) It is important that a manager or coach keep a clock so that there is no wasted time going from one station to another.

2) You may adjust the time for certain drills — three to four minutes for some versus cutting some back to two minutes.

3) It is important to have a coach or manager work with groups of players to be sure they do the drills correctly.

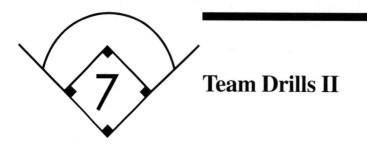

Team Drills II

♦ Purpose of Drill

To develop a series of stations to allow the defensive squad frequent repetitions of a drill in a short period of time.

♦ Equipment

Infield/outfield area

♦ Implementation

Each drill lasts five minutes

Station 1:   1) Infielders, catchers and pitchers have rundowns. Coach stands behind the pitchers and starts the drill. Also work on pitchout on squeeze play.

2) Outfielders at all bases.

Station 2:   1) Pitchers and catchers have tag play at the plate (wild pitch).

2) Pitchers direct catchers by yelling first or third. Coach stands behind the catcher and rolls the ball.

3) First baseman has low throws; breaks to the bag and sets up all types of bad throws.

4) Outfielders, middle infielders and third basemen have cutoffs and relays to third base.

Station 3:   1) Pitchers and middle infielders have pickoffs to second base. They must give the sign.

2) First basemen, third basemen and catchers have fly ball communication in front of the plate and in foul territory along the first- and third-base lines.

3) Outfielders are throwing fly balls to each other, working on getting steps down.

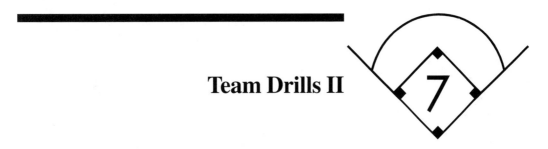

Team Drills II

Station 4:   1) Pitchers, catchers and middle infielders are throwing to second base.

2) Third basemen and first basemen are doing slow rollers. First basemen must get to the bag and set up play with a runner on second base; first basemen must keep ball in front of them on bad throws.

3) Outfielders are throwing ground balls — getting feet in position to make the throw. Spend time taking good angles but emphasizing to go get the ball.

Total Time: 20 minutes

♦ Key Coaching Points

1) It is important that a manager or coach keep a clock so that there is no wasted time going from one station to another.

2) The length of certain drills may be adjusted — five to six minutes for some versus cutting some back to four mnutes.

3) A coach or manager should work with each group of players to be sure the drills are completed correctly.

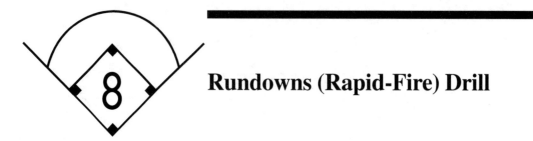

Rundowns (Rapid-Fire) Drill

◆ Purpose of Drill

To put your players in a rundown situation where they have to execute the correct technique.

◆ Equipment

Infield, baseballs, gloves and batting helmet

◆ Implementation

1) Have the pitchers line up between home and first in foul territory.

2) Have the position players (infielders) take their appropriate positions.

3) Let the outfielders and extra players divide up between first, second and third.

4) Position a coach behind the pitcher's mound with a baseball.

5) Have one pitcher at a time occupy the pitcher's mound. He will follow the throw from the coach.

6) The coach will throw to first and the first baseman will run the runner toward second and throw to the shortstop when he yells "now."

7) The shortstop will tag the runner out.

8) Then proceed to run a runner from second to third and then third to home using proper technique.

◆ Key Coaching Points

1) Make sure that the player running with the ball gets the runner running back.

2) The infielders should both be either on the inside or outside of the base lines.

3) Try to keep the throws to a runner at one or two maximum.

4) Run the drill for about five to six minutes of rapid-fire.

Rundowns (Rapid-Fire) Drill

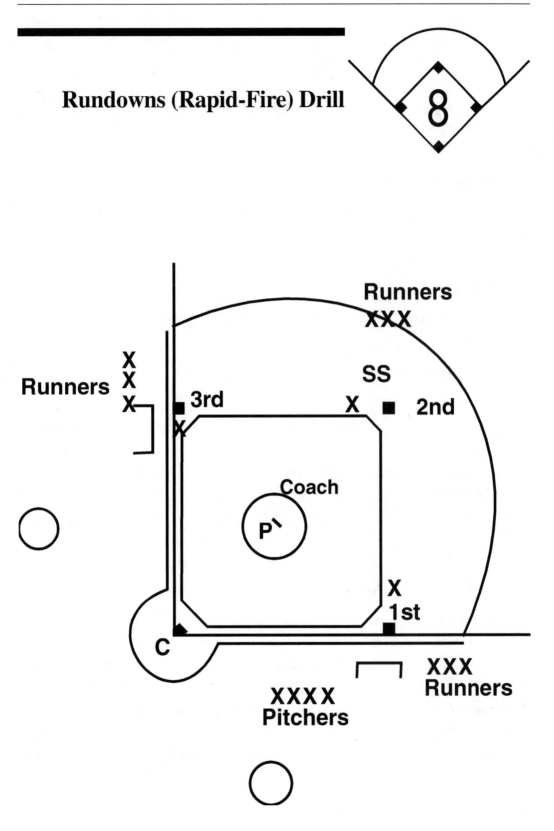

Double Cutoffs and Relays Drill

◆ Purpose of Drill

To teach and practice the proper technique in executing the double cutoff system.

◆ Equipment

Fungo, baseballs, baseball field and batting helmet

◆ Implementation

1) Put a lineup on the field.

2) Have the extra players and pitchers line up at home plate with a helmet on in the field.

3) Position a coach behind the pitcher's mound to be assured of hitting balls in the gaps.

4) Let the middle infielders run the double cutoff system while the extra players run the bases to simulate game conditions.

◆ Key Coaching Points

1) The double-cut tandem consists of the shortstop and second baseman. The trailer or second cutoff man lets the lead know where to throw the ball.

2) The distance between cutoff men is about 15 to 20 feet. The trailer is there in case the outfielder overthrows or short-hops the lead cutoff man.

3) Remind the players to keep the ball off the ground; one good throw leads to another.

4) You can put a runner on first base to work on throws to home plate or third base.

Double Cutoffs and Relays Drill

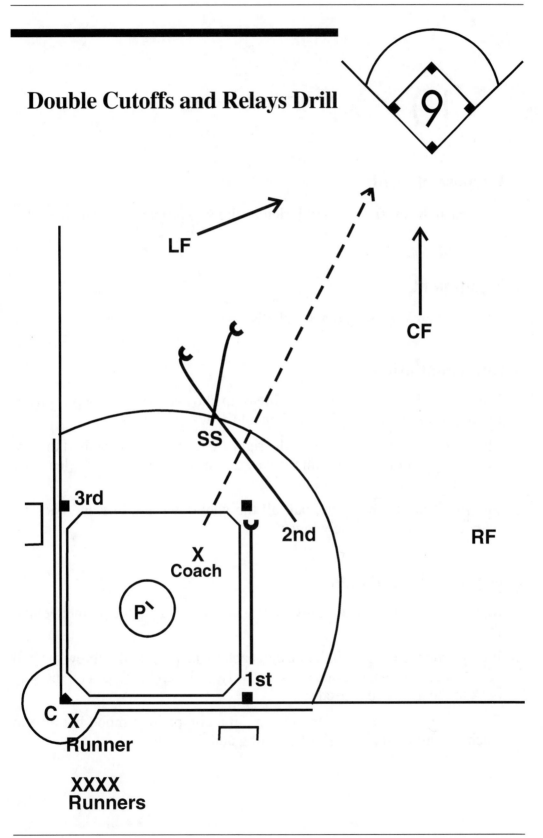

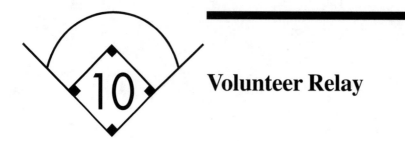

Volunteer Relay

♦ Purpose of Drill

To teach the outfielders and infielders how to properly execute the relay play.

♦ Equipment

Outfield area, grassy area, baseballs

♦ Implementation

1) Have the outfielders and infielders break up into two to three groups, spreading out from the right-field foul line all the way to center field.

2) The coach will start the drill on the right-field line having the ball thrown from one player to the next all the way to the end and back to the lead guy positioned on the right-field line.

3) The first team to throw the ball all the way down the line and back up without dropping it is the winner.

♦ Key Coaching Points

1) Make sure the players turn glove side when throwing to the partner behind them.

2) If they drop the ball, the ball must go back to the player who threw the ball and then back down the line consecutively to the end and then all the way back to the guy who started it.

3) This is a great drill to put the players in a competitive mood but also to teach the proper relay skills of catching and throwing.

Volunteer Relay

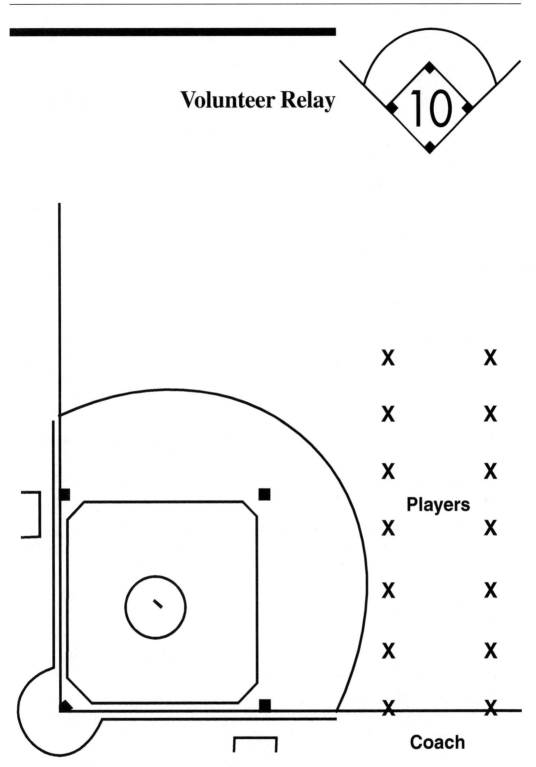

Bunt Defense Runner on First

♦ **Purpose of Drill**

To teach the defense how to properly defend against a bunting situation with a runner on first base and no outs.

♦ **Equipment**

Infield area, helmets, baseballs, bats

♦ **Implementation**

1) Have the infielders take their positions with a runner occupying first base.

2) Position the pitchers between home and first base in foul territory 15 feet off the first-base line.

3) Have the outfielders line up on the on-deck circle on the third-base side of the infield with one outfielder assuming his position in the batter's box.

4) The pitcher will kick and throw to the plate after checking the runner and cover the area in front of home plate.

5) The infielders will defend against the bunt, making sure they get at least one out, but in case of a bad bunt, such as one hit back to the pitcher, they will try to get the lead runner at second base if at all possible.

♦ **Key Coaching Points**

1) We have our catcher refrain from calling "two, two two," or "one, one, one" because we want the pitcher to hop off the mound and field the ball knowing where he is throwing the baseball.

2) The pitcher will immediately go to second base on a ball bunted right back at him. He will go to first base 99 percent of the time on anything else bunted left or right because he has no chance at second base.

3) If the ball is bunted hard down the third-base line, the third baseman will come up and throw to second getting the lead runner.

4) The key here is to get an out.

Bunt Defense Runner on First

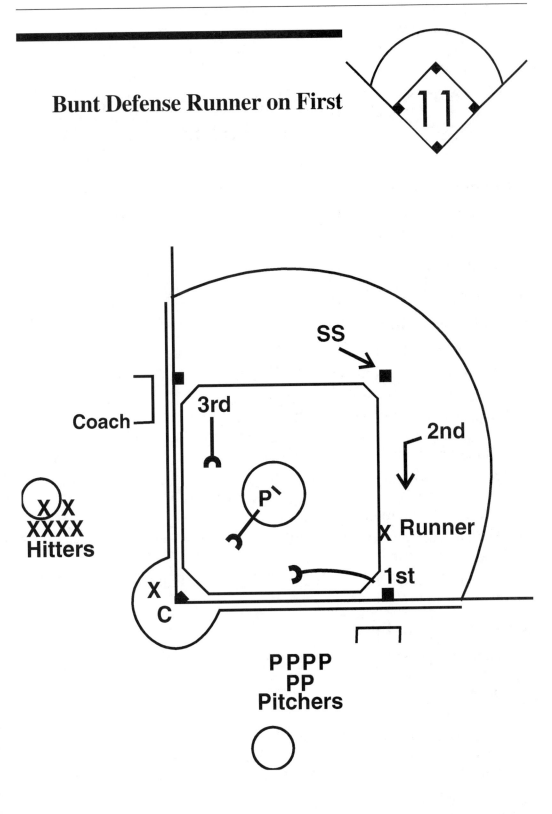

Coach

SS

3rd

2nd

P

Runner

Hitters

1st

X
C

PPPP
PP
Pitchers

Bunt Defense with Runners on First and Second

♦ Purpose of Drill

To teach the defense how to effectively defend against a bunting situation with runners on first and second.

♦ Equipment

Infield area, helmets, bats, and balls

♦ Implementation

1) Have the infielders take their position with a runner occupying first base.
2) Position the pitchers between home and first base in foul territory 15 feet off the first-base line.
3) Have the outfielders line up on the on-deck circle on the third-base side of the infield with one outfielder assuming his position in the batter's box. (If you have backup players in the infield they can be bunters in this drill.)
4) The pitcher will kick and throw to the plate after checking the runner and cover the first-base line. His responsibility is to cover a ball bunted right back toward him to the third-base line.
5) The first baseman will cover the first-base side and swing in like a banana as he breaks for the ball.
6) The third baseman will only charge on a ball bunted hard and will field it and throw to first base.

♦ Key Coaching Points

1) The pitcher must check the runner at second base on a given signal and then kick and throw to the plate to keep him from getting too big of a lead. This is a timing play with the shortstop yelling back to hold the runner at second base.
2) This is the most difficult play for a third baseman. The top priority must be to get an out. So if the ball is bunted too hard or bunted where the pitcher cannot make the play, he must charge and get the runner at first base.
3) This is a great drill that you can run for 15 minutes working on the defense, and as a team defend against a late-inning play that will be a game winner.

Bunt Defense with Runners on First and Second

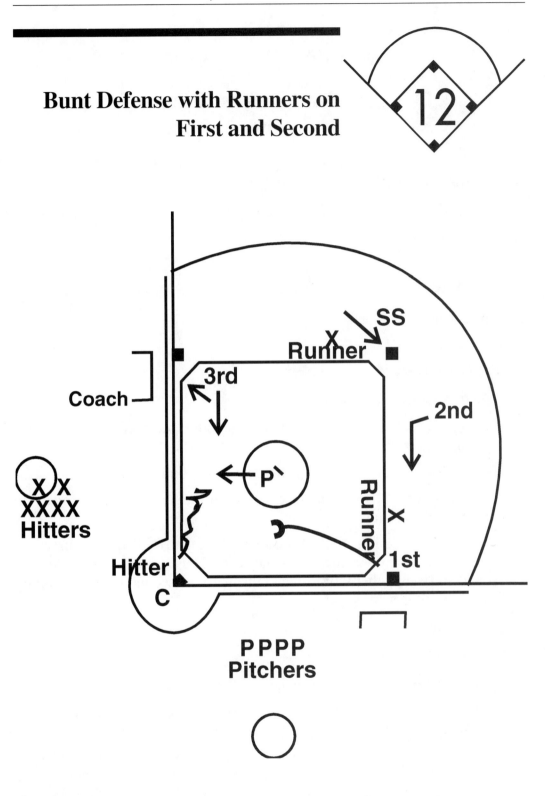

Bunt Defense Pick at Second

♦ Purpose of Drill

To practice the pickoff play at second base during a defensive bunting situation with runners at first and second.

♦ Equipment

Infield area, bats, balls

♦ Implementation

1) Infielders take their positions.

2) Have one pitcher take the mound with the other pitchers in foul territory between first and home.

3) Have the outfielders and extra infielders be the bunters.

4) Position runners at first and second with a bunter at the plate ready to execute the bunt play.

5) The pitcher will come set, the shortstop will break to third, the first baseman and third baseman will break in. The second baseman will break toward second and the pitcher will turn and throw to the second baseman hoping to pick the runner off second base.

♦ Key Coaching Points

1) This is a great pickoff drill especially if you run the crash defense.

2) During bunting practice run this play often during the series of drills to practice timing between the pitchers and the second baseman.

3) The second baseman must break to the bag as soon as the shortstop leaves his position and breaks toward third; everybody needs to move at the same time so the second baseman doesn't break too early to tip off the pick play.

Bunt Defense Pick at Second

Crash Bunt Defense

◆ Purpose of Drill

To practice executing the crash defense with the infielders breaking in from the corners; the sole purpose is getting the lead runner at third base out.

◆ Equipment

Infield area, bats, balls, helmets

◆ Implementation

1) The defensive players take their positions in the infield with one pitcher on the mound.

2) Have one pitcher take the mound with the other pitchers in foul territory between first and home.

3) Have the outfielders and extra infielders be the bunters.

4) Position runners at first and second with a bunter at the plate ready to execute the bunt play.

5) When the pitcher comes set, the shortstop will break to third, the third baseman will break in, the second baseman will go in and over, and the first baseman will break in. The pitcher will kick and throw to the plate at the same time and the defense will execute the play.

◆ Key Coaching Points

1) This play is designed for the third baseman to field the ball bunted down the third-base line and throw to the shortstop covering third base to get the lead runner.

2) Remember — get an out. If there is no play at third, go to first for an out.

3) It is important that the pitcher kicks and goes to the plate right after the shortstop breaks toward third.

4) The corners (first baseman, third baseman) almost break in at the same time as the pitcher kicks and goes to the plate to be in position to field a poorly bunted ball.

Crash Bunt Defense

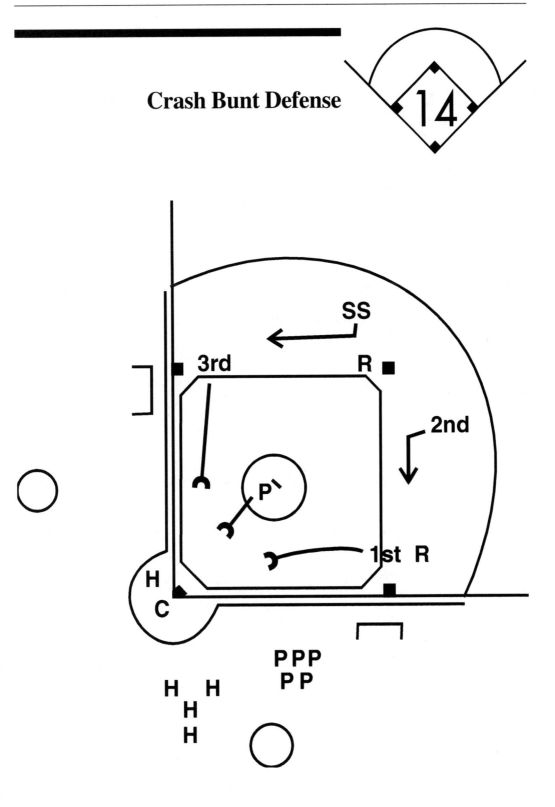

Horizontal Toss and Catch Drill

♦ Purpose of Drill

To teach the player how to track and follow a moving object accurately with both eyes, such as a ball in flight.

♦ Equipment

A juggle stick, two wands from Sports Vision Training, Harvey Ratner & Associates

♦ Implementation

1) Position a player with the wands balancing the juggle stick with three balls attached.

2) As the player flips the juggle stick in the air, the ball goes from the starting baton to the other baton as it goes for one-half turn.

3) The full turn, ball A goes from the starting baton one full turn or circle and then back to the starting baton.

4) Practice double, triple or unlimited rotations and catches.

5) Flip the juggle stick as high as you like — the higher the better for depth perception.

♦ Key Coaching Points

1) Make sure that the player starts out slowly, juggling with just half turns at first.

2) It is important that as the skill level increases the player flips it higher to work on depth perception.

Horizontal Toss and Catch Drill

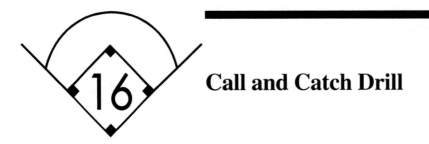

Call and Catch Drill

◆ Purpose of Drill

To teach the player how to track a specific object such as a baseball.

◆ Equipment

Sports Vision Ring by Harvey Ratner & Associates

◆ Implementation

1) Have two players position themselves approximately 10 feet apart.

2) As the player flips the ring to the partner he will call a color either before or during the toss.

3) The partner will try to catch the ball which he has called.

4) You may try to call and catch two colors as you improve.

5) To keep score: one point if you catch the correct ball, two points for catching two balls.

◆ Key Coaching Points

1) This drill helps players improve tracking ability for a specific object.

2) It allows you to focus on a specific color and then react by catching. You will notice an increase in depth perception and concentration level will continue to improve.

3) Remember, you may use one or two hands to catch the Vision Ring.

Call and Catch Drill

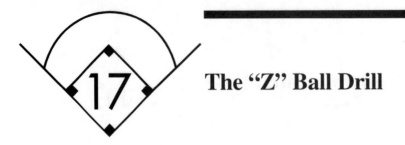

The "Z" Ball Drill

♦ Purpose of Drill

To teach the player how to develop hand-eye and eye-foot coordination.

♦ Equipment

A "Z" ball by Harvey Ratner & Associates.

♦ Implementation

1) Two partners will team up with or without their gloves approximately four to five feet away.

2) They will bounce the ball to each other, reacting to the ball by moving their feet and getting in a position to catch it both using their feet and their hands.

3) After a player catches the ball on one bounce he will bounce it back to his partner.

♦ Key Coaching Points

1) This allows the player to react to the "Z" ball which bounces left or right or up and down, and allows him to work on quickness of his hands and feet.

2) This also allows him to work on his first quick step that so many infielders need.

3) You will also notice that the player will focus in on the "Z" ball with more intensity, working on the hand-eye coordination.

4) Another option for the drill is to line up in front of a wall, bounce the ball off the wall, react to the ball and catch it.

The "Z" Ball Drill

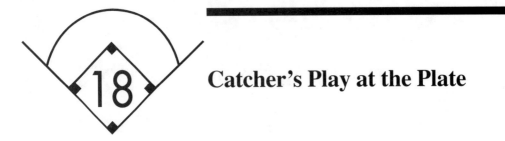

Catcher's Play at the Plate

◆ Purpose of Drill

To work on receiving throws from the outfield, making the tag at home and also working with the cutoff man with the proper communication skills.

◆ Equipment

Baseball field, fungos, bat

◆ Implementation

1) Position a coach at home plate with a fungo and his catcher ready to receive the throw from the outfield.

2) Position your third baseman and first baseman in cutoff positions ready to receive throws from the right fielder, center fielder and left fielder.

3) Use three cutoff men — one at third, one right behind the mound and one at first base.

4) Position the outfielders in their proper positions with them going in order one at a time.

5) The coach will toss a ball up and hit it to left field. The left fielder will throw it through the cutoff man with the catcher receiving the throw or using proper communication skills for him to cut it and throw to the plate.

6) The coach will then hit it to the center fielder; he will throw through the cutoff man standing behind the mound. Then he will hit to the right fielder.

◆ Key Coaching Points

1) This drill is designed to get a rapid number of throws in a short period of time from your outfielders and give the catcher practice in communication with his cutoff man and also receiving the throw and blocking the plate using the proper technique.

Catcher's Play at the Plate ⟨18⟩

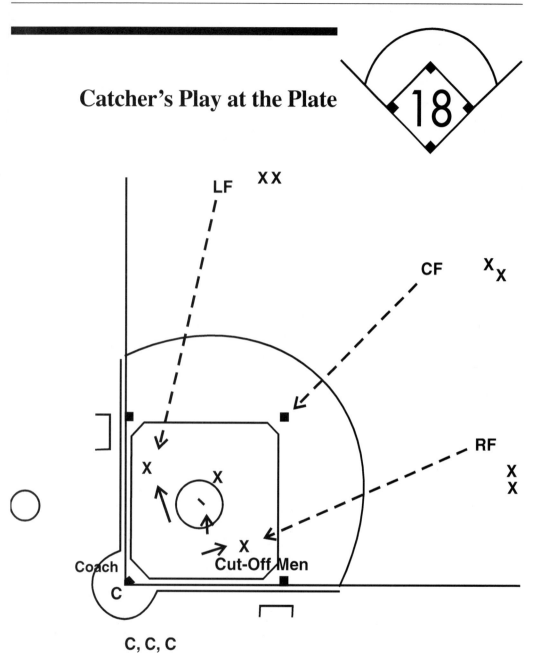

2) This drill can be used without cutoff men so that the catcher must catch everything thrown from the outfield and will also be a conditioning drill for the outfielders to throw without using the cutoff man forcing them to throw the ball all the way to the plate with one hop or all the way in the air.

3) This drill is designed so that you have several catchers rotating in. Make sure you have more than one catcher receiving the throw. The catchers will rotate at home plate receiving throws from the outfielders.